HOMESCHOOLING

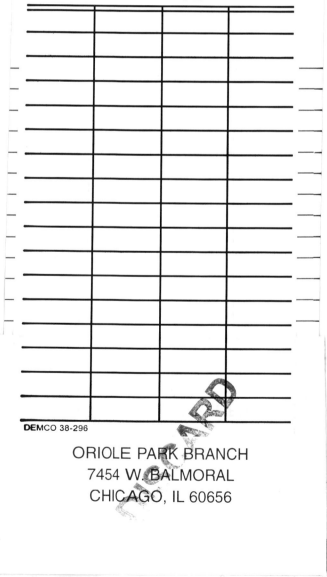

HOMESCHOOLING

— *Your* —

GIFTED CHILD

*Language Arts for the
Middle School Years*

Lee Wherry Brainerd

Introduction by Wendy Moss, Ph.D.

New York

Library of Congress Cataloging-in-Publication Data:
Brainerd, Lee Wherry.
    Homeschooling your gifted child : language arts for
the middle school years / Lee Wherry Brainerd
with Wendy Moss.—1st ed.
        p. cm.
    ISBN 1-57685-430-2 (pbk.)
    1. Language arts (Middle school)—United States.
2. Home schooling—United States.
3. Gifted children—Education (Middle school)—
United States. I. Moss, Wendy, Ph. D. II. Title.
    LC3993.27 .B73 2002
    428.1'071'2—dc21

                                    2002006833

Printed in the United States of America
9 8 7 6 5 4 3 2 1
First Edition

ISBN 1–57685–430–2

For more information or to place an order, contact LearningExpress at:
    900 Broadway
    Suite 604
    New York, NY 10003

Or visit us at:
    www.learnatest.com

ABOUT THE AUTHORS

Lee Wherry Brainerd is a local contact and counselor for California Homeschool Network (CHN), the largest inclusive group supporting homeschoolers. She writes for *California Homeschool News* and represents CHN at the annual LINK homeschool family-friendly conferences. A former teacher, she and her husband homeschool their son in Altadena, California. She is also the language arts author of *Basic Skills for Homeschooling*.

Wendy L. Moss, Ph.D., is a school psychologist in New York. In this position, Dr. Moss gives guidance to teachers and principals, as well as to parents, on ways to better meet the needs of students. She is actively involved in aiding children through individual and family counseling.

CONTENTS

HOMESCHOOLING
Your
GIFTED CHILD

Understanding Giftedness

by Wendy L. Moss, Ph.D., ABPP, FAASP

If you have decided to homeschool your gifted middle school child, or are seriously considering it, then you already know that this can be quite a complex, yet hopefully rewarding undertaking. As you talk with your friends and family, you will find that people have very different views on this topic. For instance, a pessimist might say that parents who purposely take on the additional role of educator, while also dealing with their gifted child's entrance into adolescence, are just asking for stress and high blood pressure. The optimist may inform you that you are beginning an exciting exploration of your child's potential by breaking away from the structure of traditional schooling and by tailoring lessons to your learner's intellectual gifts. The realist would generally take the middle ground.

This book is written for the realist, who looks at the benefits of homeschooling but also wants to be prepared for the challenges. This book is not meant to be a textbook or a curriculum guide. Rather, it was written with a different goal. Some creative learning strategies will be offered to assist you, the parent/educator, as you support your gifted child on the road to academic enjoyment and success. Of course, everyone has a personal view of what constitutes life success, such as meeting academic goals, enjoying social popularity, maintaining emotional health, and so on. In this resource book, the goal will be to offer you many methods and alternatives that you may employ when covering the academic topics in language arts with your gifted learner, so that the educational journey toward success will be enriched.

Upcoming chapters will address the academic issues. However, since this book is geared toward homeschooling *gifted* learners, it is important to first take some time to examine the term "gifted learner." Every day people talk about children who are "highly intelligent," "amazingly smart," "gifted," or "unusually talented." You may wonder, are these pronouncements based on a specific set of criteria or assessments, or are they merely conjecture and opinion? Is giftedness quantifiable or is it subjective? Who are these children? What are some of the definitions of giftedness? In the next few sections, an overview of giftedness and some educational implications in the middle school years will be explored.

▶ GIFTEDNESS—A GENERAL OVERVIEW

As a psychologist, I have studied intelligence and have frequently administered IQ (intelligence quotient) tests to learners. I know that no single test exists that will measure all forms of talent. The term "gifted" can be used to describe a wide range of children with different areas of strength. One such child may be a quick learner who can analyze information to arrive at novel conclusions. For illustrative purposes, let me present a brief description of eleven-year-old Ellen. Ellen's parents report that she used to become restless in class because she understood concepts that were taught within the first few minutes, then she struggled to quietly wait for her classmates to learn the same material. Ellen dreamed of becoming an inventor and often generated ideas for her ultimate creations. In addition, this young learner helped others brainstorm new ways to look at situations that initially appeared to have no easy answer. Ellen also used her knowledge of history to help her to suggest better ways to handle current world affairs. Is Ellen gifted? Yes, many people would agree that Ellen's advanced thinking in several areas is a reflection of her intelligence.

However, Ellen cannot be our only blueprint for determining if a child is truly gifted. Giftedness can be evident in different forms in different people. For instance, Joey is a very different child from Ellen, yet some people would assert that he is also gifted. Joey is an eleven-year-old boy who does fairly well in all of his academic subjects and has a wide circle of friends. Joey is admired by many adults and children because of his musical talent. Typically, he can listen to a song on the radio, then sit down at the piano and play it. While he prefers not to learn to read sheet music, he is respected for his ability to reproduce the songs that he hears. In this case, Joey is successful in his social and academic worlds. In addition, he has an unusual talent. Is he gifted? It could be argued that he meets the criteria for giftedness because of his special musical talent.

Okay, so individuals who are advanced in many areas (Ellen) and those who are more typical in development but have an area of unique skill (Joey) can all be identified, under a broad definition, as gifted. What about someone who generally struggles to master schoolwork? Could such a person be gifted as well?

There are some children who, at first glance, do not appear to be gifted in the traditional sense. A good example of this is the learner who is identified as having a learning disability, yet has a high IQ. A learning disability can be defined, for the purpose of this chapter, as an area of significant weakness relative to a learner's other abilities. For instance, a child may be very capable in most areas, but display significant delays in the understanding of mathematical concepts or mathematical calculation. A learner can become confused by having areas of both giftedness and deficit.

At times, a child may not have the confidence to pursue an area of giftedness because of feelings regarding past failures or struggles in the area of disability. Jason is a thirteen-year-old who hated studying, reading, and anything related to academic subjects. He struggled to master his studies and became quite creative at explaining why it was never a good time to do work. Jason's parents became concerned about his lack of motivation. They decided to seek the guidance of a neuropsychologist to determine the cause of Jason's emotional block.

Test results from the neuropsychological evaluation clearly indicated that Jason was an extremely gifted learner when his visual-motor skills were assessed. (More information about this area of talent is discussed in a later section.) However, he was diagnosed with a reading-based learning disability. The evaluator felt that Jason had developed frustration and anger whenever faced with any reading task. His learning disability, coupled with his emotional response to reading, effectively masked any motivation Jason might have had to pursue goals, including those within his areas of talent. Jason believed that perseverance wasn't rewarded with success, so he withdrew, even when the task would have been easy for him (e.g. a project involving his visual-motor skills). He preferred to tell everyone, "I'm stupid. So what!" Armed with the knowledge from the evaluation, Jason's parents were able to help build up Jason's confidence, emphasize his areas of giftedness, and eventually address his learning disability.

So, Ellen, Joey, and Jason seem to all have areas of talent or giftedness. What about a learner who struggles to meet *numerous* developmentally appropriate expectations? Why should anyone speak about this child in the context of this discussion on giftedness?

There are some people who may struggle in school and have trouble with higher level, abstract thinking. These individuals may have limited ability to function independently in life. However, despite these challenges, they may display one or several uncanny abilities within a narrow range. For instance, someone in this category may be able to multiply five-digit numbers by other five-digit numbers without the use of a calculator or pencil. Other individuals may be able to tell you what the weather was like on a particular day several years earlier. Perhaps this person also qualifies for the talented and gifted classification? It depends on how narrow or broad your definition is of giftedness.

At the risk of further complicating the scope of giftedness, let's also consider groups of learners who possess an area of potential talent, but who have not yet revealed it. These young teenagers may be very shy, quiet, introspective, or lacking in the perseverance to pursue an area of giftedness. In addition, there are other talented students who become so frustrated with the process of learning, perhaps because of their awareness that some information has to be memorized and/or studied, that they prefer not to face the challenges. This warrants further explanation. Many gifted children learn in an almost automatic fashion during the very early years. They may not struggle to read, write, or understand concepts. Therefore, they might miss out on the conscious development of skills that help one learn how to approach new, uncertain information and learn from it. Working hard to understand something may be a new experience for a gifted child in the middle school years. No matter how bright these learners are, there are times when they will need to focus on learning a skill or concept. When learners find this too anxiety provoking or frustrating, they may shy away from the situation or challenge rather than embrace the experience or, at least, continue to learn despite the discomfort.

For instance, a gifted ice skater will most likely skate better if she is motivated to work long hours on skills and routines that will help her improve her performance (since not all complicated moves and jumps will come naturally and immediately). When a learner is physically, intellectually, and emotionally available to learn, and to persevere, then hidden areas of talent may emerge.

▶ INFORMATION ON GIFTEDNESS

The study of unique characteristics that differentiate individuals from one another has been evident throughout history. For instance, hunter-gatherer societies had to determine who had leadership skills, who had the most physical perseverance for manual labor, and so on. In more recent times, researchers have studied the performance of individuals on scales of intelligence, have arrived at specific factors that they believe define intelligence, and have a greater understanding of some of the IQ differences that may distinguish one person from another. In this section, some of the definitions of intelligence and giftedness proposed by professionals will be explored.

Howard Gardner, a well-known Harvard educator and psychologist, has developed a theory of **multiple intelligences.** In his book, *Intelligence Reframed: Multiple Intelligences for the 21st Century* (Basic, 1999), Gardner originally identified seven intelligences in his theory of multiple intelligences. Since the time of its original conception, he has added an eighth, the naturalist intelligence. Your gifted child may fit one or many of these intelligences:

- ◆ *Linguistic intelligence* allows individuals to communicate and make sense of the world through language. Poets exemplify this intelligence in its mature form. Students who enjoy playing with rhymes, who pun, who always have a story to tell, who quickly acquire other languages—including sign language—all exhibit linguistic intelligence.
- ◆ *Musical intelligence* allows people to create, communicate, and understand meanings made out of sound. While composers and instrumentalists clearly exhibit this intelligence, so do the students who seem particularly attracted by the birds singing outside the classroom window or who constantly tap out intricate rhythms on the desk with their pencils.
- ◆ *Logical-mathematical intelligence* enables individuals to use and appreciate abstract relations. Scientists, mathematicians, and philosophers all rely on this intelligence. So do the students who "live" baseball statistics or who carefully analyze the components of problems—either personal or school-related—before systematically testing solutions.
- ◆ *Spatial intelligence* makes it possible for people to perceive visual or spatial information, to transform this information, and to recreate visual images from memory. Well-developed spatial capacities are needed for the work of architects, sculptors, and engineers. The students who turn first to the graphs, charts, and pictures in their textbooks, who like to "web" their ideas before writing a paper, and who fill the blank space around their notes with intricate patterns are also using their spatial intelligence. While usually

tied to the visual modality, spatial intelligence can also be exercised to a high level by individuals who are visually impaired.

♦ ***Bodily-kinesthetic intelligence*** allows individuals to use all or part of the body to create products or solve problems. Athletes, surgeons, dancers, choreographers, and crafts people all use bodily-kinesthetic intelligence. The capacity is also evident in students who relish gym class and school dances, who prefer to carry out class projects by making models rather than writing reports, and who toss crumpled paper with frequency and accuracy into wastebaskets across the room.

♦ ***Interpersonal intelligence*** enables individuals to recognize and make distinctions about others' feelings and intentions. Teachers, parents, politicians, psychologists and salespeople rely on interpersonal intelligence. Students exhibit this intelligence when they thrive on small-group work, when they notice and react to the moods of their friends and classmates, and when they tactfully convince the teacher of their need for extra time to complete the homework assignment.

♦ ***Intrapersonal intelligence*** helps individuals to identify their own feelings, to build accurate mental models of themselves, and to draw on these models to make decisions about their lives. Although it is difficult to assess who has this capacity and to what degree, evidence can be sought in students' uses of their other intelligences—how well they seem to be capitalizing on their strengths, how cognizant they are of their weaknesses, and how thoughtful they are about the decisions and choices they make.

♦ ***Naturalist intelligence*** allows people to distinguish among, classify, and use features of the environment. Farmers, gardeners, botanists, geologists, florists, and archaeologists all exhibit this intelligence, as do students who can name and describe the features of every make of car around them.

Source: Harvard University's Project SUMIT: Schools Using Multiple Intelligence Theory, www.pz.harvard.edu/sumit/MISUMIT.HTM

Parents who apply this theory work to incorporate language, numbers, nature, social activities, sound, and body movement into the leaning process.

Here is another take on intelligence from the manual for the *Wechsler Intelligence Scale for Children—Third Edition (WISC-III)*, an intelligence test that school psychologists often utilize to measure their students' abilities. In his Preface, Joseph Matarazzo states that early on, Wechsler "discerned that intelligence is a global capacity of the individual and that it is the product of both the individual's genetic makeup, on the one hand, and the individual's socio-educational experiences, drive, motivation, and personality predilections, on the other hand" (p. iii). In the introduction to the WISC-III manual, the nature of the test is explained briefly; it reads, "Consistent with Wechsler's concept of intelligence, the subtests of the WISC-III have been selected to tap many different mental abilities, which all together reflect a child's general intellectual ability" (p. 1). However, even within the manual, it is noted that many factors, including emotional stressors, can have an impact on test results. To summarize, this suggests that intelligence is not a simple factor that can be quickly measured and that abilities can be affected by any combination of physical, emotional, social, educational, environmental, or genetic factors.

Furthermore, in an article, "Intelligence: Knowns and Unknowns," published in *American Psychologist*, the authors describe Robert Sternberg's 1985 "triarchic theory." This theory proposes that there are "three fundamental aspects of intelligence—analytic, creative, and practical" (p. 79). They go on to explore Jean Piaget's views on intelligence, noting that Piaget believed that "[i]ntelligence develops—in all children—through the continually shifting balance between the assimilation of new information into existing cognitive structures and the accommodation of those structures themselves to the new information" (p. 80). Piaget's developmental theory suggests that the thinking process is one that changes over time as a learner matures.

Intelligence and giftedness are topics that have been discussed and written about in many books and articles, and intelligence proves to be a multidimensional concept with many varied definitions—from including only learners who are globally advanced to a broader meaning including children who display a narrow range of talent. Human beings are complex in nature, so intelligence, talents, and giftedness are not narrow concepts with easy definitions.

Do you have a clear definition of giftedness now? In the upcoming section, examples of giftedness will be highlighted. If you identify your learner in these pages, consider ways to foster her area(s) of talent when developing curriculum and when reading through the rest of this book.

▶ MORE DETAILS ON WAYS A LEARNER CAN BE TALENTED OR GIFTED

Giftedness or a highly developed talent can distinguish one child from many others. The gifted learner typically has a level of knowledge, sophistication, or skill that is considered to be within the top 1–2 percent of the population of individuals of one's own chronological age or peer group. Another way to define this is to say that they fall at the far, upper end of the bell-shaped curve. It is important to note that learners' interests may or may not overlap with their areas of talent. For instance, thirteen-year-old Peter loves basketball and plays on a team in a civic league. He watches college and professional basketball on television and loves going to games. Despite this significant sports interest, Peter's actual skills are considered to be only average or slightly above average in running the court and shooting the ball. Therefore, Peter has a specific interest in sports but not an unusual gift in this area. Perhaps one can argue that his persistence in studying the game is a talent. This is something that will be explored shortly.

Earlier, a few definitions were offered for general giftedness. However, one can create an extensive list of possible areas of specific talent. You may already know that your child has an unusual skill. There are numerous areas that can be considered talents or areas of giftedness, such as advanced abilities in expressive language, receptive language, visual-perceptual skills, visual-motor skills, athletic skills, processing speed, convergent and divergent thinking skills, creativity, memory skills, executive functions, self-motivation, emotional maturity and social skills, smell and/or taste discrimination, written language, reading comprehension skills, and mathematics skills. These areas will be explored in the next section, with the goal of helping you create academic lessons that may be tailored to fit your learner's talents, resulting in a more meaningful education.

In the traditional classroom setting, there are typically a few students who are described as "always needing to talk." These learners sometimes raise their hand throughout a lesson to add additional information or to personalize the material to their own experiences. A child who is highly verbal may have a talent in the area of **expressive language**. These learners are not just verbal, but skilled communicators. At times, they actually clarify their own understanding of a lesson by talking about it. For instance, some children with this area of talent may benefit from taking time to retell the message of a story or poem. By using their own words, the lesson's meaning is reinforced. A person talented in expressive language skills may gain a more thorough understanding of the lesson by reteaching the lesson to another or by engaging in a debate with another about the topic. For example, Clara read an article about the quality of her neighborhood's water system. Clara initially concluded that the water system should remain pure, without any added chemicals. When she and her older brother debated the issue, Clara's parents asked her to take the opposing view. Clara reread the article, gathered more information from the Internet, then passionately used her verbal skills to create a powerful argument. Through the debating situation, Clara was able to think about both sides of an issue that was creating tension in her community. Without the added benefit of debating the issue, Clara was initially certain that her one-sided view was the only one with merit.

As a parent/educator you may want to utilize debating as a way to help your child utilize expressive language skills to more fully understand concepts. However, it is important that the debate remains in the realm of the topic of study and that respect for the other's opinion is maintained—in other words, that the debate doesn't become one of parent vs. adolescent. Both of you will probably have enough personal debates over the years without debating in the home-classroom setting.

Some learners may not be able to succinctly retell or verbalize their understanding of material, but they have an acutely developed skill in the area of **receptive language**. Simply, this can be looked at as the flip side of expressive language. Expressive language is what the learner articulates, while receptive language is how the child understands the statements and comments made by others. For instance, Billy is a competent reader, but he prefers to have others read to him. When asked about his preference, Billy explains that he is able to engage in the learning process more easily when someone else talks to him about the lesson as he learns it. While this may just be Billy's preferred learning style (auditory), it has been shown that when he listens to others teach lessons, he actually quickly, though quietly, grasps higher-level concepts and material that would ordinarily be geared toward students at a more advanced developmental level. For Billy, his area of giftedness can be utilized to help him overcome emotional obstacles to his learning process. For instance, at one point, Billy was refusing to learn poetry, claiming that it wasn't real literature. His parents left him alone in the living room and went to talk with each other in the next room. They purposely left the door open and spoke loudly. Billy's parents spoke to each other about the topic of poetry and the special messages that this form of literature can communicate. Billy, no longer needing to be argumentative, learned a lot by eavesdropping. This was a creative way to bypass Billy's resistant attitude at that time and to help him to be available to the learning process. His parents effectively tapped into his comfort in listening to discussions and Billy was able to quickly grasp the lesson utilizing his receptive language skills.

The previous example shows a somewhat dramatic case. Let us assume that your child is usually motivated to engage in academic activities. Your learner, who has a receptive language talent, may feel more comfortable learning by listening to lectures on tape, books on tape, or by actually attending age-appropriate seminars on particular topics. Even if this approach is one that facilitates rapid learning for your child, it is still important to also teach in a multi-modal fashion so that your learner becomes comfortable absorbing information in many different manners. Flexibility of learning allows all of us to be able to adapt better to a variety of situations in which others will not always gear activities to our personal learning style or giftedness. This is true for any child, with any area of specific interest or talent.

Next on the list of possible forms of giftedness, you can find one that is referred to as exceptional **visual-perceptual skills**. For your learner, this can include such abilities as: being able to discriminate between two similar visual images, being able to quickly discover what is wrong with a picture, having a keen understanding of why photographs with different shading impact the gestalt of the picture, and/or an appreciation of paintings and sculptures. While these learners may be *visual learners*, this area isn't just a preference but a talent. These learners may learn best when you add visual material to lessons. In the early years, a child with this area of giftedness may begin to truly understand the importance of time by developing photographs in a darkroom. The child can see that the same negative looks subtly to dramatically different if exposed to the developing process for a brief versus a longer time period. The concrete visual example of time can be very helpful to this learner who quickly grasps visual information.

The child who is talented in **visual-motor skills** has two areas that, in combination, form this kind of giftedness. The learner with visual-perceptual talent, as just described, may have an acute visual sensitivity and ability to be keenly visually alert. In visual-motor skills there is the added motor component. For instance, Rachel was able to surprise and delight her family when she, as a three-year-old, made a complicated structure out of Legos. A year later, she visualized how she wanted a garden to look and, with some help from her mom and dad, eventually planted the seeds and witnessed her dream become a reality. Jim, a ten-year-old, drew his own comic strip series, with only minor guidance on his spelling from his father. Stephanie, age fifteen, followed a blueprint and made a lamp. These learners tend to have advanced fine-motor skills along with a keen visual/perceptual ability. Constructing a lamp, like Stephanie did, or building another object can allow the child to understand the value of fractions (while imparting the indispensable skill of following instructions.) For instance, if two pieces of wood are supposed to be identical to support a structure, having one 36 inches and another 36¾ inches could mean the difference between a stable and unstable product.

Athletic skills also involve both visual and motor components and are often described as tapping *gross motor abilities*. A soccer star, for example, must view the field, determine the placement of the players on both teams, make an educated guess about where each player is headed, then have the physical skills needed to negotiate the soccer ball past the opposing team. Athletes may have either fine-motor (small muscle group) or gross-motor (larger muscle group) skills. Sometimes they have both. A learner with an athletic talent may learn other material through this gift. For instance, looking at baseball scores (hits, walks, runs) can turn into a mathematics lesson. A discussion about the angle of one's best pitch could be equated with geometry concepts. In addition, the complexity of combining various actions (e.g., eye-hand coordination, timing of swinging the baseball bat, running speed) and repetition of practicing techniques to become a top baseball player can be compared to the top essay that must include the nitty-gritty, detailed work (research, editing, revision, proofreading) to have a finished, professional-quality product.

Processing speed is also an area that is often equated with intelligence. However, the specific information processed can vary from one learner to another. One child may quickly process the direction of a sound, another person may quickly look at a brainteaser puzzle and arrive at a method for solving it, while another individual may quickly grasp a new lesson. In some of the formal tests of intelligence (such as the *Wechsler Intelligence Scale for Children, Third Edition*), some tasks are timed to ascertain not only the child's ability to master an item, but also the child's ability to master it under a time pressure. Students who are quick processors may need less time to complete certain work. However, just because a student quickly processes, say, a word analogy question, it does not necessarily mean that understanding other concepts will come as rapidly. Jorge rapidly completes puzzles and grasps scientific concepts. In contrast, he needs more time to understand grammar concepts. In this case, Jorge's processing speed gift is specific to certain areas of learning and thinking.

At times, a child is impulsive and quickly finishes assignments or tasks. If the end product is haphazardly completed and does not display the learner's best efforts or level of reflection, then speed does not constitute a gift, but rather an area for discussion. Speed along with successful mastery are *both* important for this form of giftedness. This brings up an important point: as the parent/educator, please resist the urge to condense lessons into shorter time frames and cover many topics in the course of a day simply because you understand that your learner can process information quickly. Some children think intensely and rapidly but require more frequent breaks. This is where the balancing act, between focusing on intelligence and emotions, becomes so important. As the parent and the teacher, you are uniquely able to determine the most suitable way to meet the multitude of needs that your learner has.

A strong ability to think in both divergent and convergent manners is another area that can be considered a talent or part of giftedness. **Convergent thinking** is the ability to determine how various objects or events are similar. For instance, a learner may be able to draw comparisons about how words that appear to look so different actually follow similar rules. In addition, your child may be able to draw parallels between historical situations that preceded wars.

On the other hand, **divergent thinking** skills reflect a learner's ability to determine how a single event, object, or word can be looked at in different ways. The learner may be able to generate numerous uses for a typical household object, such as a stick of gum. Young children often are called "creative" when they can utilize their divergent thinking abilities to make a piece of candy into a warrior or a pencil into a phone. Inventors may also display their unique divergent thinking skills when they take common materials and create a novel product. Learners who have advanced divergent and convergent thinking skills may be able to find several ways to communicate an idea, but can also narrow down ideas to arrive at the most common feature.

Creativity taps into divergent thinking skills and may be viewed as a specific area of giftedness. Creativity comes in many forms, such as talent in the performing arts, musical endeavors, ability to arrive at novel conclusions by synthesizing new and old information, and the ability to problem-solve and arrive at a unique way to resolve a dilemma. A child who is talented in singing, but struggled early on with reading skills, may benefit from singing the words aloud initially. The actor may bring to life a character from a book by trying to identify with that character and understand the subtle nuances of being that person in the historical or fictional time of the story. A problem-solver may enjoy brainteasers that require the use of logical inference and creativity in order to arrive at a conclusion. Creative learners may ask to complete an assignment in a way that deviates from our own ideas of how it should be done. If your learner can explain the rationale behind the creative approach, and it is educationally sound, then supporting the idea also can support your child's belief that venturing out and offering unique thoughts to others is worthwhile.

Memory skills are a vital part of our functioning, since individuals build on prior experiences as they grow and learn. Some learners have amazing gifts to remember factual information. For instance, Sam may be able to recite all the states at 24 months of age, while ten-year old Sheila may be able to spontaneously tell you the birth and death dates of all the American presidents. Alexandra is a different learner. While she doesn't have the advanced memory for concrete facts, she is able to vividly remember events that have occurred in her own life. Therefore, there are many components to memory and many ways that children can be talented in their memory skills. Memory is not a single skill, and it involves many different steps and cognitive operations. First, a student needs to immediately remember information just learned; then he needs to begin to store it for a longer duration; then he will need to consolidate it into long-term memory; later be able to retrieve it. At times, a student has one part of this process mastered but struggles in another area. For instance, a learner may have no problem listening to a phone number, then going to the phone and dialing it. However, if that same learner is asked to retrieve the number from memory a few hours later, it may be difficult or impossible. Memory is multi-faceted. Some memories are auditory, visual, tactile, or olfactory (associated with smell). If you think back to your own recollections of situations, there are times that you may vaguely remember a trip to someone's house but have a clear recollection of the smell of something baking in that house. A learner who remembers information best by storing it through tactile (or touch) channels, may benefit from being able to touch and manipulate the materials in the lesson. Many math lessons can be taught utilizing objects to highlight points. For learners with an extremely accurate, detailed memory (sometimes labeled as a photographic memory), they may look at a page in a book and may not need to reread it when studying or reviewing the information. Rather, the learner may just need to reflect on the image that has been imbedded into memory.

An important part of any learner's success is to have well-developed **executive functions**. These include planning skills, impulse control, the ability to pay attention, and the ability to organize tasks. If your child excels in these areas, it makes learning most lessons a little easier. A student with this area of talent can display more initiative and independence when completing projects and will likely gain self-esteem and self-confidence in the process. Similar attributes of motivation—being a self-starter, being curious, with a thirst for knowledge are characteristics that can generalize to most academic lessons as well as life lessons.

For **self-motivated** learners, parents need to be careful about giving external rewards (for example, a gift for completing a good project) because the learner may begin to feel that the effort was really for the reward, not for the joy of the journey. Curious children need teachers to expose them to the various lessons, but then their **curiosity** and thirst for knowledge should help guide them through the maze toward mastery of the topic. If your curious learner isn't burdened by self-inflicted, undue pressure to succeed and learn, and can still work within the confines that society sometimes imposes (for example, a tour guide at a museum cannot always stop to answer all of the questions posed by a particular patron), then the drive toward independence and self-learning can be one to encourage and foster.

In recent years, society has certainly witnessed the fact that childhood is not always carefree and that children sometimes have serious emotional struggles. A child that has advanced **emotional maturity** and **social skills** is a learner who is better prepared to weather the frustrating periods in life. The ability to cope with stress and the ability to empathize with others are valuable skills in personal as well as professional success. If your child has the emotional tools to overcome obstacles and frustration, this will help the learning process. Learning involves being receptive to information that may not have been presented earlier. If a learner only feels comfortable exploring topics that have already been mastered, then the learning process can be rocky. The emotionally mature learner may verbalize some discomfort with a new lesson but can focus the needed energy on the learning process and not on the anxiety of not knowing all the answers immediately.

A few other areas of giftedness are worth mentioning. Some children have keenly developed **smell discrimination** and/or **taste discrimination**. For instance, John can tell when his mother varies the amount of onions used in a particular recipe. Is this talent useful? Certainly if one aims to become a chef, then this skill is extremely useful. It can also be helpful in the learning process. For instance, a lesson in chemistry can utilize the combination of various food condiments to drive home the point that the end product can be greater than the sum of its parts.

Some learners have gifts that are directly related to academic work. The child who has a talent in the area of **written language** may be encouraged to vary the form of writing (such as memoir or poetry) to generalize the gift to many areas of written language. The child who has advanced **reading comprehension skills** might be encouraged to read and discuss many forms of literature. However, it is always important to remember that a learner may have advanced reading skills but not advanced emotional maturity. Therefore, book selections must consider both factors. Please turn to Appendix C to access Lee Wherry Brainerd's reading list suitable for gifted learners. The **math whiz** could utilize this talent in everyday life. For instance, one activity could be to calculate how much money should be saved each week in order to get the "must have" videogame. Whenever lessons can be fun for the learner and also practical to the everyday lessons of life, then two important goals have been accomplished—academic growth and life preparedness!

The list of specific talents and gifts can go on and on. The important point is to highlight the fact that no two gifted or talented children fit one mold or profile. Therefore, you should interpret the information provided to you in upcoming chapters in the context of your particular child's areas of giftedness and needs.

▶ IQ Testing

So far, the previous sections have examined the complexities of defining the term *giftedness*. Next, the pros and cons of IQ testing will be explored. There are numerous IQ (intelligence quotient) tests out there and each test assesses a variety of different skills and abilities. Since there are too many areas of potential talent to tap in one test, intelligence tests focus on assessing skills that provide "the best predictor of academic achievement" according to Prifitera and Saklofske in *WISC-III: Clinical Use and Interpretation.*

If a learner has already displayed unusual talent in one or more areas, why would anyone want to give such a child an IQ test? There are many reasons, but three are especially important to review in the context of homeschooling.

(1) The first reason is that IQ tests may be helpful in the evaluation of why a gifted learner displays significant difficulties in some academic areas. For instance, Ramon is a twelve-year-old who easily grasps most concepts, is very athletically coordinated, and loves anything to do with science. In addition, Ramon is articulate and can create wonderful bedtime stories for his younger brother. Despite these numerous areas of strength, Ramon's written language skills are below average. His letters are immaturely formed, he often fails to space between letters, his sentences are poorly sequenced, and spelling and punctuation are problematic areas for him. Ramon's parents asked a local psychologist to administer an IQ test to Ramon to clarify his areas of relative strength and weakness. The evaluator found that results of IQ testing, along with achievement testing, revealed that Ramon had a superior level of intelligence with learning disabilities in the areas of graphomotor functioning (i.e. handwriting) and written language. These results were helpful in the later development of specific techniques to teach toward Ramon's strengths and to help him compensate for his areas of difficulty. Earlier, you read about Jason, who was rebelling against schoolwork because of an underlying reading-based disability. Both Ramon and Jason (and their parents) were relieved to learn that they truly are bright, despite areas of challenge.

There are many areas where bright children may struggle. In fact, if you reflect on the potential areas of giftedness outlined earlier, you may find that some areas of strength and one or more areas of weakness or significant delay describe your learner. If you suspect that your gifted child may have an area of concern, where can you turn? It's always a good first step to check with your pediatrician to make sure that your learner isn't suffering from a physiological difficulty (e.g., hearing loss causing difficulty listening; lead poisoning causing inattention). After that, the public schools, hospitals, clinics, and private practice psychologists/neuropsychologists will often have the capability to administer IQ testing along with other specific assessments tailored to your area(s) of concern for your learner. A gap between IQ and achievement on specific tasks often is reason for further inquiry and possible intervention and remediation to address your child's areas of relative weakness. Any evaluator you seek should be appropriately credentialed in your state to administer intelligence tests.

While the topic of gifted children with areas of disability is a complex and important area for discussion, this book focuses more on your learner's strengths—specifically in language arts. While it is important that areas of relative weakness are not overlooked, this book's goal is to help you to creatively teach toward your learner's talents. Even when areas of disability need to be addressed, it is important to also reinforce your learner's areas of giftedness.

(2) If you do not believe that your child has an area of significant delay or weakness, why else would you want to have your learner complete an IQ test? A second reason is that IQ tests typically tap a number of different cognitive areas, such as visual memory skills and/or verbal comprehension skills. Therefore, test results can reveal a learner's areas of relative strength. Even if a learner has a globally strong intelligence profile, there may be some areas that are more developed than others. As the person responsible for guiding your child's educational program, this information can allow you to tailor teaching to your learner's strengths and preferred learning style.

(3) Another reason why an IQ test is important to consider for your child is that it may be required in an application process for admission into certain gifted programs. For instance, if a gifted program needs to screen children on some uniform measure to determine which learners fall in the 98th percentile or above on a scale of general ability, they may rely on a standardized IQ test. Even though you teach your child at home, you may want to consider some of the programs that are offered to gifted children. These programs may have the benefit of supplementing your educational plan—offering your learner a chance to socialize with other gifted learners—and the courses may be geared toward your child's areas of interest (such as history, poetry, or physics). While some gifted programs are ten-month schooling experiences, others are designed so that classes meet only on weekends or during the summer. If you are considering such a program, the admissions office can let you know the requirements for eligibility and the specific tests that might be necessary to determine whether your learner qualifies for admission.

At times, a child's specific areas of talent may not be evidenced on a formal IQ test. For instance, cooking ability, athletic talent, or musical skill may not be revealed on a test of intelligence. If you feel that your learner should be allowed to attend advanced courses or training in these specific areas, it might be more helpful to contact the specialized schools and plead your case than to simply submit results of intelligence tests that do not reflect your child's areas of giftedness.

▶ IQ Tests—Factors That May Negatively Impact Your Learner's Test Results

There are many factors that can affect a child's ability to perform optimally on a test or task. Since an IQ test is administered at a particular time and in a particular place, any factor that negatively impacts your learner on that day and time can affect the test results. In this section, a few of the possibilities that may cause a tester to perform below expectations will be reviewed, including: atypical answers due to humor or a desire to be seen as unique; mistrust of the examiner; refusal or reluctance to guess at answers; motivation or effort; impulsivity; low frustration tolerance; distractibility; processing speed; perfectionism; depression; anxiety; and physical challenges or medical issues.

Here's a closer look at a few of these factors.

Giving atypical answers. Learners are often encouraged to think creatively and to generate novel ways to look at a situation or problem. However, if a child does not understand that sometimes a more traditional answer is expected, then this may affect scores on the IQ test. For instance, if a learner enjoys giving atypical answers because of a desire to be seen as unique, a symptom of anti-authority rebellion, or because the learner is trying to be funny, this may lead to scoring deductions on the test. Here is an example to help illustrate this point. Marco is asked to determine how to fit a certain number of large machines into a particular room, and his atypical answer is, "That's easy. Just stack the machines on top of each other or build an extension to the room." Depending on the type of machines, stacking them may not be appropriate, since they may need to be easily accessible for the people working on them. Extending the room may also not be practical because of financial or building-code restrictions. Regardless of the feasibility, the question assumes that the test-taker would stick to the confines of the dimensions given for the room. Margaret's conventional response, which listed the dimensions of each object, the dimensions of the room, and how arranging the machinery in particular places in the room would allow all of the equipment to fit in and be effectively available for use, is the type of response that the IQ test would look for. Being able to give a direct answer to a specific question is a skill that is important on many assessments, including standardized intelligence tests.

Being uncomfortable with, or mistrustful of, the examiner. Most people perform better when they feel encouraged by those around them. It is a well-known fact that athletes perform better with the home crowd cheering them on during competitive sporting events. If your learner feels uncomfortable with, or mistrustful of, the examiner, then this could create tension and negatively affect concentration and confidence. It is important to make sure that the examiner is well trained and is able to make your child comfortable in the testing situation. For example, Patrick appeared to be fine the morning of the test, but his father noticed that he became moody as the time for the examination approached. By the time Patrick entered the testing room, he was complaining of a stomachache. Patrick typically experienced stomachaches when nervous. The evaluator noticed that Patrick avoided eye contact and that he complained that he was not up to taking the test. The evaluator knew that many youngsters were nervous before tests, and he thought that this might be true for Patrick. After approximately ten minutes of talking about the test and establishing rapport by talking with Patrick about his favorite interest, hockey, Patrick stated that his stomachache wasn't really hurting too much and he could begin testing. Sensitive examiners will routinely take some time at the start of the evaluation to establish rapport.

Being uncomfortable with risking an educated guess. A child may be comfortable with the examiner but still be uncomfortable taking risks during the testing experience. Many intelligence tests do not penalize a child for guessing at an answer. It is often better to risk an educated guess rather than simply saying, "I don't know." If a child hesitates to offer answers unless there is 100% certainty that the response is correct, he may lose points by not offering that correct guess. Willingness to guess at answers involves a learner having the confidence to risk failure and confidence that taking educated guesses will reflect positively on him or herself. Mohamed found himself uncertain about how to answer some questions on the test. He initially told the examiner, "I'm not really sure how to answer that question." After the examiner told him that he could feel free to offer any answer that he thought might be accurate, Mohamed complied. While Mohamed did not always earn points for all of his guesses, he did score accurately on a number of items despite his initial uncertainty about the answer. At the beginning of the testing session, it might be helpful for the examiner to spend some time talking with your child about whether guessing at answers is appropriate for the particular test in question.

Lacking motivation and effort. Motivation and effort are important in life for all people, even those who are highly gifted. Without taking the time to reflect on questions and to do one's best, your learner is likely to score lower on the IQ test than if motivation and effort are both high. Tests of intelligence typically present test-takers with many questions or problems. Therefore, the answers may require problem-solving skills, time to contemplate strategies to solve the task, and so forth. If a child embraces each item as a challenge and perseveres until item mastery is achieved (or until it becomes clear that, despite the best of efforts, the problem cannot be solved by your learner), then your child can leave the testing situation feeling pride at having given the examination 100% effort. Hank had the ability to put minimal effort into many academic subjects and still excel at them. When he began taking the intelligence test, Hank quickly answered many items, but did not put forth much effort as the task demands increased. The evaluator wasn't sure if Hank was lacking motivation or if he was lacking knowledge. The evaluator spoke with Hank about his perceptions of the test. Hank and the tester began a 20-minute discussion about how important it was for him to show his capabilities in the variety of different tasks being assessed. Hank liked the evaluator and thought that the test did require more energy, so he began to exert more effort to perform well. The evaluator noted a dramatic improvement in the quality of Hank's responses.

Exhibiting impulsive behavior. Some students are quite motivated to do well on an IQ test, yet they answer quickly and do not spend time contemplating the questions before responding. If you know that your child tends to be impulsive, then it may be helpful to have a discussion about patience and the benefits of taking one's time before giving answers on tests. Some students believe that speed of response is the priority rather than accuracy. When a test-taker learns that some parts of the IQ test are timed, this may reinforce the misconception that time is the priority. Some gifted learners can respond quickly *and* accurately when their talents are emphasized, but they need to realize that this fast-paced approach to answering test items may not always benefit them. Erica was motivated to do well on the test and felt that she was trying hard to give answers, but she wanted to impress the evaluator by giving her responses quickly. The evaluator suggested that Erica should try to respond as fast as she is able, but only after she feels that she can produce her best response. Erica liked working quickly, but she did begin checking her answers before stating that she was done with the task. This helped ensure that she did not produce inaccurate answers because of impulsively rushing through the work. Depending on the task, the test-takers may need to be patient with themselves and allow time for reflection about the question or problem.

Demonstrating low frustration tolerance. Even gifted learners will find that some test items are challenging. If your learner has a low frustration tolerance—that is, difficulty tolerating a frustrating task—then this could affect the way your child responds during the IQ test situation. For instance, Chris has quite advanced mathematical calculation and reasoning skills, yet, he often yells at those who try to teach him new math concepts. He verbalizes his belief that math should always come easily to him and he shouldn't have to spend time trying to solve a problem or trying to learn a new aspect of this academic subject. (On rare occasions, he became so frustrated and angry that he literally left his desk and walked away from the stress.) If Chris similarly feels angered by, or frustrated with, portions of an intelligence test, because the items require sustained effort and time, then his emotions may rob him of energy to stick with the task and display his cognitive abilities.

Showing distractibility. Attention and concentration are two factors that are quite important as children age and their work requires more attention to details and more sustained concentration. Children with an Attention Deficit Hyperactivity Disorder (ADHD) sometimes display such significant distractibility that educators struggle to find ways to hold their focus long enough for concepts and lessons to be taught. Even learners without the disorder may display short attention spans. Michael, for instance, loved sports, video games, and anything with speed and action. He often daydreamed about these interests when he was supposed to complete his academic work. When Michael became distracted during testing, he had to be reminded to tell the examiner when he needed a break from the work and that he should work hard to remain focused while testing progressed. Michael had the ability to concentrate, although he sometimes lacked the interest in the activity and preferred to briefly withdraw into his own thoughts. If you realize that this describes your own learner, you may want to share this information with the examiner prior to the testing meeting. At times, the examiner may allow breaks (e.g., bathroom breaks; a break to walk around; a break for a snack) to give the examinee the best chance of performing in such a way as to accurately reveal cognitive abilities with minimal negative impact from distractibility.

Measuring processing speed. Some learners receive praise because of their deliberate, methodical style of approaching academic and life lessons. As noted earlier, the IQ test may assess your child's processing speed. For instance, Lisa displays a slow and deliberate (and accurate) response style during testing. The correct responses will be scored, but the rate of response may not allow Lisa to earn the maximum points for timed items. Generally, the examiner can easily identify this pattern of responding and note it in a report.

Expressing perfectionism. Perfectionism is another characteristic that may negatively impact your test-taker. A high motivation to excel and to do well is an important component of a success formula. However, sometimes that motivation becomes so intense that a learner is dissatisfied with anything but perfection. Perfectionism can be counter-productive, as shown by students Carolyn and Joan. Carolyn spends hours completing a poetry assignment and then has no energy or time to address other tasks. Joan has a more severe difficulty with perfectionism and may never even complete the poem because it is never viewed as "good enough." A perfectionist may also frequently encounter frustration, since no one is entirely perfect. On the IQ test, a perfectionist like Joan might refuse to offer educated guesses if the accuracy of the response is not guaranteed. Or, she may check and recheck answers so many times that all benefits of working quickly (such as points for speed of task completion) are lost.

Being depressed. Sadness, grief, or depression can lead to temporary psychomotor retardation (slower responses), difficulty concentrating, apathy, and a tendency to overlook details. If this describes your child, you may want to consider postponing the intelligence testing, unless the information is important to rule out other causes of the depression (e.g., neurological/physiological disorders). In adolescents, depression can include symptoms of sleep and appetite disturbances, hopelessness, helplessness, apathy, lethargy, low self-esteem, withdrawal, and other symptoms of sadness. However, some depressed learners actually seem agitated rather than lethargic. Dawn's parents noticed that she had become "hyper" at the age of fourteen. She had difficulty sleeping, was often irritable, and concentration deficits were evident. Her parents thought that Dawn may have an Attention Deficit Hyperactivity Disorder. Dawn met with a psychologist for an evaluation. The evaluator determined that Dawn's symptoms emerged after her boyfriend broke up with her. Dawn was diagnosed with depression. She promptly received effective treatment. If you are questioning whether your learner is depressed, share this concern with someone trained to evaluate emotional difficulties and disorders. Depression sometimes lifts without medical or psychological intervention, but it can lead to more serious concerns, such as suicidal thoughts or actions. In regard to IQ testing, scores can be significantly deflated because of depressive symptoms. If it's essential that your learner be evaluated during this emotionally difficult time, the results may be interpreted as accurate for your child while in a depressive state, but may not be an indication of underlying intellectual ability.

Being anxious. Emotions can seriously impact a child's availability to learn and to perform tasks. Adolescence, with the many identity and hormonal changes that occur, is a time when learners may go through numerous stages and moods. Anxiety can lead to similar testing concerns as those just described for the depressed adolescent. A test-taker who is anxious may rush through work, have difficulty concentrating on the work, or fear taking risks and offering educated guesses. Nick, for example, was so nervous about taking the IQ test that his primary goal was to get it over with. He rushed through the work, felt his heart pounding as he encountered difficult items, and he just wanted to run out of the room. Nick knew that his mother expected him to take the testing seriously, so he tried to focus on the work. However, his anxiety impeded his ability to concentrate. If your child's anxiety is specifically identified as test anxiety, then a good evaluator may offer you some hints that you could use, before the day of testing, to help your learner relax and see testing as a nonthreatening situation. Also, the evaluator may be able to spend some time with your child, before formal testing, to help ease tensions.

If anxiety is more pervasive than simply arising when your child is placed in a testing situation, then this is something that may be more challenging for the examiner to address. However, it would still be helpful to review your child's emotional issues with the person who administers the IQ test. Any time a child is tested despite emotional turmoil, the results need to be looked at as having been obtained while the test-taker was in a particular emotional state. A thorough evaluator will document, perhaps in the behavioral observations section of the report, any overt evidence of anxiety that your learner displayed during the evaluation.

What if your learner is emotionally content, trusts the examiner, is not distractible or impulsive, and enjoys the testing process? Is there any other concern you should consider? The mind and body are not distinct and independent parts of a learner. Therefore, if your child is struggling with a medical or physical issue, this could impact IQ testing scores as well. A typical example is the overtired child. Russell returned from camp on a Wednesday, stayed up late to tell his parents about his adventures, and then had difficulty falling asleep in his own bed after a few weeks away. The next morning, Russell was awakened early to have a leisurely breakfast and prepare for the trip to the evaluator's office. Russell had only three hours of sleep but appeared to be energetic and ready for the testing experience. His parents felt that he was going to be able to perform up to his potential because he seemed to have energy and have a positive attitude about the evaluation. Unfortunately, Russell's lack of sleep did impact his concentration. The evaluator noted concentration difficulties but could not determine how significant this factor was on test scores.

Other **physical and medical concerns** should also be considered when scheduling testing. A child who is just getting over the flu may seem back to normal, but may still become easily fatigued. A child who is taking a new medication may not react in a typical fashion when asked to concentrate and problem solve. Certainly vision problems or hearing problems may impact test scores.

At times, it is important to obtain IQ scores *because* of a physical difficulty. Melody was in the hospital awaiting surgery to remove a brain tumor. She was a gifted learner in a school for gifted children. Despite earlier testing, the surgeon wanted information on Melody's cognitive functioning level immediately prior to surgery so that he could review any changes that the tumor may have caused. He also wanted to be able to use the results as a baseline for post-surgical evaluations. In this situation, the IQ testing was used to monitor Melody's cognitive status, not to assess her overall abilities in optimal circumstances.

There are many more ways that physical, social, and emotional issues can impact your child, and thus, any assessment results. IQ testing scores are likely to be influenced by significant life events or circumstances that impact your learner's ability to learn and perform.

▶ SHOULD IQ SCORES BE SHARED WITH YOUR LEARNER?

There are pros and cons to sharing IQ scores with your child. First of all, IQ testing does not evaluate all areas of functioning and it would be important for a learner to truly understand the usefulness and meaning of the scores. At times, having the information that one is gifted can increase motivation, confidence, and energy to excel. After learning his test results, Malik commented that "I didn't know that I was so smart. I guess I could probably do well if I try." Edward had previously lacked self-confidence and felt that his sibling was the smart one in the family. He had avoided schoolwork and put his energies into athletics. After learning the results of the evaluation, Edward continued to participate in sports, but he also turned some of his energy toward his academic work.

When Abby learned that she was extremely gifted, it helped her to understand why she sometimes felt different from her peers. Abby had thought it was because she was "weird" or that there was something wrong with her. After the IQ test results were explained to her, Abby's parents noted that her self-esteem was higher and she appeared to be more relaxed.

There are several important cautions to note about sharing IQ results with your adolescent. Some children react in the complete opposite fashion from the way Abby responded to the information. Some gifted children feel that an objective evaluator diagnosed them as different. This can be a painful experience for some adolescents, who work hard to blend into the group. A gifted learner may need some education on the fact that being gifted, or even exceptionally gifted, does not mean that peers will reject them or that they can't participate in, and enjoy, everyday activities. The test just reveals information on a learner's thinking patterns and cognitive abilities.

Another caution to sharing test results can be illustrated by fourteen-year-old Charles. After he learned that he was intellectually gifted, Charles felt that he must be superior to all of his classmates. Prior to IQ testing, Charles was frequently excluded from social get-togethers and was rarely invited to parties. The other children in the neighborhood preferred sports activities to Charles' interest in literature and politics. After obtaining the IQ scores, Charles announced to his peers, "I don't care if you don't want to hang out with me. I'm a genius and I don't have time for you people." Obviously this defensive statement did not make Charles popular and Charles was even more excluded by others.

Some learners actually display increased levels of frustration after IQ test results are shared with them. Many children have a notion that if you are truly bright then everything should be learned immediately and easily. This is a fallacy, but the gifted student may become more frustrated with himself each time a lesson takes time to be learned or after a project is not perfect at its completion. If you notice this change in your learner, it is important to discuss the concept of intelligence. After all, the learning process is one that everyone must go through and, at times, it can take time to learn challenging concepts even if one is gifted.

Another reason to be cautious with sharing IQ results is, at times, a learner responds to the information about giftedness by assuming that there is no longer any need to put effort into work since "I'm so smart anyway." The student may look at lessons in certain subjects as unnecessary since "I'll be rich and successful even if I don't learn this stuff." Since effort is an important ingredient to success, a child who reacts in this way will need some guidance on the importance of effort despite high intelligence.

▶ RISKS AND BENEFITS OF YOU KNOWING YOUR CHILD'S IQ SCORE

Receiving information about your child's cognitive profile and overall IQ scores may help you to develop curriculum that is geared to your learner's gifts. For instance, if your child displays strong long-term factual memory skills, learning new material may make more sense when it is tied to some information that had been taught or experienced earlier. Donna had gone on a family trip to China several years ago. Now, at the age of thirteen, Donna appeared to be disinterested in history. She often said, "These people aren't alive, so why should I care about them anyway?" When Donna was able to reflect back on her previous trip and how she had learned many facts about ancient leaders, and their effect on present-day China, Donna was able to use this memory to convince herself that learning American history is also important to understand America today.

Despite the benefits that IQ test scores can provide, there are potential drawbacks and pitfalls to knowing your child's results. A parent who is also the educator will need to guard against being unduly influenced by the information when developing a learner's educational plan. It is important to be aware of the potential issues that might arise after you become aware of your child's IQ. At times, for instance, a parent believes that a child is quite gifted because of talents in one, or in several, areas. However, the IQ test may not reflect the talent(s) and also may not provide the high IQ score that had been anticipated. It is important to continue educating the child in generally the same manner in which growth had previously been displayed, rather than reevaluating perceptions and lowering expectations. Alex's parents learned this lesson the hard way.

Alex had always been a precocious child with a talent in the area of written language. His parents educated him at home and developed a stimulating, fast-paced, program for him. Alex thrived on the attention and loved the projects and essays that he was asked to complete. While he protested against mathematics lessons, he excelled in this subject as well. After taking an IQ test, Alex attained a score in the high average range. His parents felt that they had misjudged their son and they began to simplify the lessons. Alex was soon bored with the pace and with the content of his work and became distracted. Luckily, his parents did not take this response as confirmation that they needed to simplify lessons further. Instead, they realized that they knew their son's learning style and had to gear the curriculum to his overall abilities and not just to an IQ test score. Once Alex was challenged again, his concentration improved.

Sometimes a parent learns that a child's IQ is actually higher than anticipated. In these situations, expectations may be raised and parents might expect more comprehension and production from their learner. Once again, a child is more than an IQ number. By increasing the work demands, a child may feel emotionally overwhelmed. In fact, Jane said, "My parents think I'm smart now. They decided to torture me with more work. I wish I didn't take that test." It's important for educators to always balance a child's intellectual abilities with his or her emotional needs. If a gifted adolescent feels that the workload or expectations are too high, it sets the stage for possible withdrawal from the parent or rebellion.

▶ EDUCATING THE GIFTED LEARNER

Perhaps the ideal educational plan would be one that is tailored to the individual, fosters individuality, while simultaneously helping the learner adapt to the world. According to Susan Winebrenner in her book, *Teaching Gifted Kids in the Regular Classroom*, "Gifted students should spend most of their learning time on tasks that are more complex and abstract than those their age peers could handle" (p. 5). In their article, "Grouping Gifted Students: Issues and Concerns," which appeared in *Gifted Child Quarterly* in 1992, J.F. Feldhusen and S.M. Moon concur with this perception. Furthermore, Feldhusen, in a 1989 article for *Educational Leadership* entitled, "Synthesis of Research on Gifted Youth," also noted that "Gifted and talented youth need accelerated, challenging instruction in core subject areas that parallel their special talents or aptitudes" (p. 10).

As you will see, there are times when a gifted student benefits from moving through curriculum topics quickly. However, there is often a benefit to staying with the subject but looking at it in greater depth or from a variety of perspectives. Some learning strategies to help you as you educate your learner will be presented in upcoming chapters.

▶ BEYOND INTELLIGENCE—SOME KEYS TO SUCCESS

Earlier, key factors that could negatively impact a child's IQ test scores were reviewed. But what can enhance a learner's ability to flourish? Daniel Goleman believes that one's emotional abilities are so important to one's life that he named his book *Emotional Intelligence*. No matter how gifted a particular child is, there are personality and emotional characteristics of a learner that enhance and promote greater success. This section will review the following factors: self-confidence and self-esteem; self-reflection and social skills; motivation to learn; curiosity about the world; perseverance; concentration skills; organizational skills; creativity; ability to use unstructured time; and emotional health.

If learners feel confident in their ability to take on challenges and succeed, then they are more likely to embrace the educational process. If a child has **self-confidence** and **self-esteem**, then the initial uncertainty that can emerge when learning a new topic or concept will, hopefully, not be threatening to the learner's sense of self and self-esteem. For many learners, confidence also allows them to voice their initial understanding of the lesson, even though they may not be certain of the accuracy of their comments. This feedback is useful for the educator, since lessons can be adjusted based on the level of understanding that the learner exhibits.

The capacity for **self-reflection**, or the ability to think about one's own personal characteristics, strengths, and weaknesses and see oneself in both a subjective as well as in an objective manner, is an asset. Unfortunately, some children are accidentally taught to misperceive themselves and to set unrealistic expectations about their place in the world. For instance, Ted was always given the message that he was "the best child any parent could ask for" and that he was "probably the brightest child in the world." If Ted believes this, then it could be quite distressing when another learner comes along who has an area of talent greater than Ted's. Some learners will deny the evidence rather than believe that parents might be giving them misperceptions about themselves. Other children will begin to mistrust parental statements. While children need to feel special to their parents, it is important for them to also know that they may be viewed differently by the outside world.

Self-reflection is important in developing **social skills**. As a child becomes a teenager, the peer group tends to take on more significance. Knowing when to stop a monologue, interact in a dialogue, or actively listen to others is a skill important for acceptance from others. In general, turn-taking, having empathy, knowing that another's feelings are important to consider, and having the ability to relate to a wide variety of people are all useful skills for later success.

If you have decided to homeschool your child, it is also important to provide social experiences where your learner can socialize with same-aged peers. Social learning, social modeling, and identification with one's peer group can be learned most naturally in an authentic context. Adolescents typically move toward independence, which tends to involve separating from their parents and forming ever-changing bonds with peers. Offering your child the chance to experience unstructured as well as structured group activities can help foster the social skills that are so important for this transition period and for later life.

Energy to devote to the learning process, another asset, can simply be broken down for this discussion as involving **motivation to learn** and **curiosity about the world**. In science, it is often found that new research develops after scientists question accepted hypotheses and risk exploring alternative explanations for situations. The curious child is one who is generally open to learning and interested in the lessons. Even gifted learners, however, may accept the world in a passive manner and lack the spark of curiosity that propels independent desires to learn. On the other hand, some adolescents who have trouble with authority question everything, but use the questions as a part of their rebellion rather than using them in a growth-oriented, productive manner. As your child's parent/educator, it might be helpful to encourage questions about lessons, but also to ensure that the questioning is productive and adds to the educational activity.

Perseverance is the ability to stick with a task long enough to succeed or to give it the best of efforts. This characteristic, along with **concentration skills** and the ability to **organize** one's work space and develop a study plan, are skills that can increase a child's ability to show areas of strength and understanding of information, as the learner moves through the learning experience. A gifted child who loses assignments, pencils, forgets what to do, or is daydreaming may be less available (although not necessarily less fundamentally competent) to conquer life's tasks.

Some of the most valuable lessons that can be learned are not formally taught. For instance, **creativity** is often nurtured in an educational setting, but developed as a learner utilizes **unstructured time** to create and imagine. Watching very young children playing, it is often apparent how much they rely on their imaginations in their play with trucks, dolls, and other toys and found objects. The early adolescent will have had many years to develop the basic skills for creative thinking, but now may need help to feel comfortable risking exposing the novel thoughts to others. Poetry is a good example of how a person combines formal schooling (e.g., defining poetry) with the ability to look at an ordinary object or the world through unique eyes.

One's **emotional health**, as described earlier in this chapter, can significantly impact many areas of functioning. If a child, for instance, is suffering from depression or anxiety, the energy and interest may not be channeled easily into academic work. An interesting drawback to a gifted learner's ability to assess situations in many ways, is that sometimes such learners can creatively find many, many reasons why they are inadequate, why they should have a low self-esteem, why the world is a terrifying place to live in, and so on. Depression and anxiety can follow from such negative contemplations. Bright teenagers can often find arguments to quickly discount the attempts by adults to make them feel better about themselves or safer in their world. If these emotional issues persist for a few weeks or result in significant changes in your child's mood, then it is recommended that your child have the chance to consult a mental health professional.

▶ BRIGHT BUT NOT "A LITTLE ADULT"

Before concluding, it is important to spend a few moments to highlight the fact that gifted children are different than *little adults*. On some levels, they may understand adult concepts and even have a greater knowledge of a particular topic than some adults in their world. However, this does not mean that they all want to be treated like adults or that they benefit from such treatment. For instance, twelve-year-old Marvin loves being included in adult conversations. His parents were accustomed to his presence as they entertained their own friends at the house. One night, Marvin went to sleep and had a nightmare. He woke up sweating and felt his heart racing. He ran to his parents' room and awakened both his mother and father. After talking for awhile, Marvin confided in his parents that their talk about a teenager's abduction and murder, in their discussion about the death penalty earlier that evening, had terrified him. His parents were surprised by this reaction, especially since the murder had not even occurred in their state. Marvin taught them a valuable lesson. He was intellectually capable of following the conversation, but not emotionally ready to process and handle it.

On this topic, it is also important to remember that even a bright, precocious child can benefit not only from protection from some of life's stressors, but also from limits. In fact, fair limits often provide a sense of security and a belief that the adults care. This writer once had the honor of listening to two teenagers talking about this issue. The first teenager bragged that he "snuck out of the house" without his parents knowing. The second teenager sighed and said, "I don't have to do that. My parents don't care what I do." Parenting is a difficult job. When do limits become so restrictive to a child that they rebel and when do permissive rules backfire? This issue is one that every parent will probably be faced with at one time or another, but may be even more confusing for the parents of gifted children who seem to be *little adults*.

▶ EDUCATING YOUR GIFTED LEARNER

The upcoming chapters will explore creative strategies to assist you as you educate your learner in the broad ranging area of language arts. As you read through the pages, consider that you will need to apply the information to your child's homeschooling program based upon your learner's intellectual talents and emotional needs.

▶ REFERENCES

Feldhusen, J.F. (1989). Synthesis of research on gifted youth. *Educational Leadership*, March, 6–11.

Feldhusen, J.F. & Moon, S.M. (1992). Grouping gifted students: issues and concerns. *Gifted Child Quarterly*, 36 (2), 63–67.

Gardner, Howard. *Intelligence Reframed: Multiple Intelligences for the 21st Century* (New York: Basic Books, 1999).

Goleman, D. *Emotional Intelligence* (New York: Bantam, 1995).

Neisser, U., et al. (1996). Intelligence: knowns and unknowns. *American Psychologist*, Vol. 51 (2), 77–101.

Prifitera, A. & Saklofske, D., eds. *WISC-III: Clinical Use and Interpretation: Scientist-Practitioner Perspectives* (New York: Academic Press, 1998).

Wechsler, D. *WISC-III: Wechsler Intelligence Scale for Children—Third Edition* (New York: The Psychological Corporation, 1991).

Winebrenner, S. *Teaching Gifted Kids in the Regular Classroom* (Minneapolis: Free Spirit, 2001).

1

Challenges and Opportunities

*Y**ou probably don't** need anyone to tell you that it's a challenge to parent, teach, or be a gifted child! Gifted-ness is sometimes difficult to define, and it is widely misunder-stood. In an institutional school setting, gifted kids may not be appropriately identified, appreciated, or nourished. Educator Stephanie Tolan claims, "Schools pro-vide too little challenge for the development of extraordinary minds. . . . Attributes that are a nat-ural aspect of unusual mental capacity—intensity, passion, high energy, independence, moral rea-soning, curiosity, humor, unusual interests, and insistence on truth and accuracy—are considered problems that need fixing."

Stephanie Tolan's oft-quoted speech "Is It a Cheetah?", which can be found online at www. giftedbooks.com/aart_tolan.html, develops the metaphor of a cheetah to describe a gifted individ-ual (both can be fast, unique, and flashy). She continues by saying that gifted children and their families often feel like "cheetahs in lion country." Tolan adds: "Many gifted children sit in the [tra-ditional] classroom the way that big cats sit in their cages, dull-eyed and silent."

Perhaps these are some of the reasons you have chosen to homeschool. You may have already been homeschooling for some time, or you may be just starting out on this exciting journey. In either case, while homeschooling a gifted child is definitely a challenge, the array of opportunities home-schooling reveals is astounding:

◆ You, as your child's guide, can adapt a curriculum to your learner's strengths, weaknesses, and pace—adding time for exploring, daydreaming, resting, and recharging.

◆ You can practice—as you and your learner deem them appropriate—acceleration, differentiation, compacting, and enrichment (all to be described later in the book).

◆ You have the lucky opportunity to mix and match homeschooling styles: unschooling, home-based, mentoring, eclectic, school-at-home, apprenticeship, Carschooling®, distance learning, and so on.

▶ GIFTED TRAITS

Since gifted children are very different from each other, there is no single ability to look for. Dana is math smart, while Caroline has an outstanding memory, and Evan plays the piano like a maestro. Remember also—as noted by Dr. Moss in the Introduction—that a child's greatest gifts might be outside the academic world's definition of achievement. For example, after one hearing, Michael mimics any sound or voice, producing uncanny impersonations.

You may recognize some or many of the following characteristics of giftedness in your own bright child. You will find that some traits *usually* apply, some *often*, and some *never*.

Check any items that usually or often apply to your child:
- ❑ enjoys or prefers to work or play independently
- ❑ can multitask—concentrate on two or three activities at once
- ❑ prefers the company of older kids and adults to that of children his/her own age
- ❑ loves to read or look through books
- ❑ reads books and magazines geared for older kids and adults
- ❑ shows interest in cause-and-effect relationships
- ❑ learns quickly and applies knowledge easily
- ❑ shows an unusual grasp of logic
- ❑ has an advanced vocabulary for his/her age
- ❑ seems extremely precocious—talks or thinks like an adult
- ❑ enjoys making discoveries on his/her own and solving problems in his/her own way
- ❑ likes to play with words
- ❑ resists conforming
- ❑ shows asynchronous (uneven) development—may be advanced in one or more areas, but delayed in others, or delayed emotionally or socially
- ❑ loves math games and figuring out how to solve math problems in unique ways
- ❑ wants to know the reasons for rules and the reasons behind the reason(s)
- ❑ discusses or elaborates on ideas in complex, unusual ways
- ❑ sees many possible answers to questions or solutions to problems

- ❑ loves to know and give reasons for everything
- ❑ is extremely curious, asks a lot of questions, and questions the answers
- ❑ shows leadership in organizing games and activities and in resolving disputes
- ❑ has a long attention span for things that interest him/her
- ❑ becomes so involved that he/she is not aware of anything else
- ❑ has unusual hobbies or interests
- ❑ has a vivid imagination
- ❑ invents games, toys, and other devices
- ❑ thinks of new ways to do things
- ❑ likes to create by drawing, painting, writing, building, experimenting, storytelling, or inventing
- ❑ excels at singing, playing an instrument, dancing, or pantomime
- ❑ responds to music, is able to improvise tunes and rhythms, or composes songs
- ❑ sees patterns and connections that others don't see, even among things that are apparently unrelated
- ❑ argues or debates about the logic of ideas, rules, or actions
- ❑ tends to rebel against what is routine or predictable
- ❑ has a well-developed sense of humor
- ❑ absorbs the speech patterns and vocabulary of different people and imitates them
- ❑ is very active; has trouble sitting still
- ❑ likes to discuss abstract ideas like God, love, justice, and equality
- ❑ expresses unusual sensitivity to what is seen, heard, touched, tasted, and smelled
- ❑ shows sensitivity to the feelings of others and considerable empathy
- ❑ expresses concern about world problems such as endangered animals, racism, pollution, and poverty
- ❑ is frustrated by imperfection in others and in himself/herself
- ❑ is extra sensitive to criticism
- ❑ shows a willingness to follow intuitive hunches even if they can't immediately be justified
- ❑ demonstrates high energy, focus, and intensity

Source: Joan Franklin Smutny, founder of the Center for Gifted at National-Louis University, *Stand Up for Your Gifted Child* (Minneapolis: Free Spirit Publishing, 2001)

Meeting Your Learner's Needs in Intellectual Development

What are your learner's special needs? The president of the World Council for Gifted Children, Dr. Barbara Clark, outlines the following needs for intellectual development in gifted children:

- ◆ to be exposed to varied subjects and concerns
- ◆ to be exposed to new and challenging information about the environment and culture
- ◆ to be allowed to pursue ideas as far as their interests take them
- ◆ to encounter and use increasingly difficult vocabulary and concepts
- ◆ to be exposed to ideas at rates appropriate to the individual's pace of learning
- ◆ to pursue inquiries beyond allotted time spans

Clark asserts that all of these needs can be met easily and inexpensively through a curriculum based on books and reading. If you add group discussions within your family, book group, or home-schooling support group, you will be meeting these other needs:

- ◆ to have access to intellectual peers
- ◆ to share ideas verbally and in depth
- ◆ to have a longer incubation time for ideas
- ◆ to pursue ideas and add new ideas without forced closure or products demanded
- ◆ to draw generalizations and test them

Teaching Language Arts to Your Gifted Homeschooler

Language arts is defined as reading, writing, listening, speaking, and the study of literature. That may seem to cover everything, but we may also add research, problem solving, and reasoning skills; vocabulary and etymology; and the conventions of the English language, such as grammar, punctuation, and usage. For good measure, let's throw in proofreading, revising, and editing. All such competencies may stand under the language arts umbrella.

The exciting thing about the study of language arts is that it touches all subjects: literature, history, current events, science, information technology, math, the social sciences, the arts, and so on. Keep in mind, then, while considering the language arts goals defined in this chapter, that you and your homeschooler have the freedom to draw upon all subjects and many modes of study.

Language arts for the gifted can be modified and expanded in a multitude of ways. The next few chapters will offer up a smorgasbord of exercises and activities that are especially designed for gifted learners of all learning styles.

Gifted learners often crave challenge. Here are eight general ways to adapt language arts—and, in fact, any subject—to the eager mind:

1. **Concrete to abstract.** Bright learners benefit from tasks that involve abstract materials, ideas, or applications. *(Jon diagrams a wedge to understand mechanical advantage in the building of the pyramids.)*

2. **Simple to complex.** Gifted learners benefit from tasks that are complex in research, issues, problems, skills, or goals. *(Rebekah figures that her volunteer work on Mitzvah Day will aid her temple, her neighbors, and a local hospice, while fulfilling her community service goals.)*

3. **Basic to transformational.** Smart learners benefit from tasks that require transformation or manipulation of information, ideas, materials, or applications. *(Applying his ideas on color and movement, David transformed his dream into a pointillist painting à la Georges Seurat.)*

4. **Fewer facets to multi-facets.** Bright learners benefit from tasks that have more facets or parts in their directions, connections within or across subjects, or planning and execution. *(Renata laid out her tree house blueprints next to the kite design, so she might incorporate the two.)*

5. **Smaller leaps to greater leaps.** Gifted learners benefit from tasks that require greater mental leaps in insight and application. *(Now that they had moved the desk, Tina wanted her daughter to figure out how to move the much larger entertainment center.)*

6. *More structured to more open.* Smart learners benefit from tasks that are more open in regard to solutions, decisions, and approaches. *(Ramiro's father thought he would try Ramiro's creative ideas to get the cat to swallow the medicine.)*

7. *Less independence to greater independence.* Bright learners benefit from greater independence in planning, designing, and self-monitoring. *(Debbie enjoys planning and coordinating her week of studies, field trips, and errands.)*

8. *Quicker to slower.* Gifted learners will sometimes benefit from rapid movement through subjects or tasks. At other times, they need a greater amount of time with a given study so they may explore the topic in greater depth and/or breadth. *(Aunt Karen saw that Tess wanted more time to absorb the museum's exhibit on triceratops.)*

GIFTED-SPEAK

Many homeschooling families do not find terms such as *acceleration, compacting,* and *differentiation* relevant, since parent/teachers already modify each subject to each child's intelligence, interests, gifts, and pace. However, if your bright child has been enrolled in a gifted program, camp, or summer school, you are most likely familiar with these "gifted-speak" terms.

Acceleration. Moving quickly through easy material or skipping material that is already learned or known intuitively. *(Nadya skipped the introduction on rhyming and went right to composing sonnets, as she was a natural poet.)*

Enrichment. Replacing or extending the regular curriculum with projects that focus on higher-level thinking skills, such as analytical thinking, logic, and problem solving.

Enrichment includes creative arts, supplemental classes, apprenticeship, independent study, distance learning, and mentoring. *(When Mavis finishes her chores, she is allowed to spend an hour at her favorite logic problem-solving website.)*

Differentiation. Adapting a curriculum to meet a student's individual needs. *(Ted's mom eliminated the "busy work" in the geography unit she had bought Ted at the curriculum fair.)*

Differentiation may comprise any or all of these components:

1. **compacting**—compressing material into a shorter time frame
2. **novelty**—introducing a novel area of study or an independent study project
3. **complexity**—encouraging the learner to explore relationships or different points of view, or use various approaches
4. **depth**—challenging the learner to delve deeper into a subject
5. **individualization**—allowing the pursuit of the student's own interests and passions

▶ GOALS FOR LANGUAGE ARTS LEARNING

The next four chapters of this resource guide, define, and detail four generic goals for language arts study. The content of these chapters is further explained later on in this chapter.

Why Care About Goals?

Why do we, as educators and parents, set goals for language arts learning? Here are six reasons that will influence your learner as he or she goes out into the larger world.

Loving Learning. The love of discovery often drives success in schooling, in the workplace, and in the world. As gifted learners demonstrate and deepen their understanding across academic disciplines, the ability to use skills such as analysis and self-expression greatly enhances the joy of learning.

Solving Problems. Gifted learners are often able to recognize and investigate problems, then formulate and propose solutions supported by reason and evidence, becoming problem solvers for life. Solving problems demands that students read and listen, comprehend, ask and answer questions, convey their own ideas clearly through written and oral means, and explain their reasoning. In all fields—language arts, math, science, social studies, and others—the command of language is essential to reason through problems and to convey results.

Communicating. Communication is the essence of language arts, and the ability to communicate effectively is essential in this Information Age. Individuals and groups exchange ideas and information—oral and written—face-to-face, in newspapers and magazines, through radio and television, and online. From the simplest "Yes, ma'am," to the most complex technical manuals, language is the basis and the joy of all human communication.

Using Technology. Many gifted children use technology with ease. Language arts actually helps us explore technology—using computers and networks to access information, be in touch with the experts, prepare documents, process ideas, and communicate results.

Working in Teams. In sports, the workplace, the family, and around the world, teamwork requires skill in the use of language. Gifted kids, like all of us, need to speak with clarity and listen well as they share ideas, plans, and instructions. In bringing outside information to a team, our kids must be able to search, select, and understand a variety of sources. Those who can read, write, speak, and listen well are valuable contributors in any setting where people are working together.

Making Connections. Different aspects of language arts are interconnected, of course: Reading and writing provide the means to receive and send written messages. Likewise, listening and speaking enable us to receive and send oral information. Speaking and writing are the creative components, while listening and reading are the receptive components of language.

Now let's explore how to measure your gifted middle schooler's progress in reaching the goals of language arts studies.

► MEASUREMENTS FOR HOMESCHOOLERS

Whatever approach to homeschooling you exercise, you will want to measure and record your student's progress. However you evaluate your gifted student, records will provide an overall picture of progress and the satisfaction that progress brings. There are multiple ways to assess your child's work, as you will read in the next section. You may want to evaluate your child's work considering:

- ◆ effort put into the project (your child's honest appraisal on this one may be more appropriate than yours)
- ◆ mastery of the material
- ◆ the finished project, if there is one
- ◆ ability to apply or translate what is learned
- ◆ progress toward the family's academic goals

Some families combine traditional measurements with less conventional "thinking-out-of-the-box" methods. This is your prerogative as a parent/educator.

Traditional Assessments

Traditional assessments include:

Grades: A, B, C, D, F, and Incomplete; or Excellent, Good, Satisfactory, Not Satisfactory; or a percentage (95%); or a fraction ($\frac{17}{20}$). Homeschoolers usually keep traditional grades in a file. Some homeschoolers give weight to this kind of grading, some do not. Interestingly, state education codes usually do *not* require grades, just an assessment of progress. To find out about the requirements in your state, visit the Home School Legal Defense Association at www.hslda.org.

Test scores: Scores from quizzes and tests found online, in workbooks and textbooks, in courses, on software programs, and on standardized tests.

Teacher or mentor evaluations: Subjective evaluations of the student's effort, outlook, work, progress, goals, and final projects.

Out-of-the-Box Measurements

Gifted kids are often out-of-the-box thinkers, and homeschoolers are experts at finding imaginative, unorthodox methods of assessing those kids' achievements. This includes subjective assessments and acknowledgment of mastery, such as this homeschooling mom's journal entry: "Luisa researched and discussed her understanding of the building of the Brooklyn Bridge. She designed an alternative suspension bridge, and wrote an essay on engineer and designer John Roebling."

The learning style (or styles) of your bright middle schooler may not lend itself to easy assessment in the traditional sense. (Turn back to pages 4–5 for more on Howard Gardner's Learning Styles.) In that case, you might measure progress in the basic skills of reading, writing, speaking, and listening using one of these creative methods:

Conversation and discussion. An informal method of measurement, but excellent experience for listening and speaking skills. Listen to your child talk about what she/he has learned and "reflect back" what has been said, to verify it. Then have your child listen to your observations and reflect them back to you.

Learning contracts, calendars, and lesson plan books. These tools should list tasks completed and ongoing. Learning contracts are especially effective for gifted learners who are self-starters or who like to work independently. A sample learning contract is on page 51.

Scrapbooking, journals, and diaries. Help your gifted middle schooler keep records of and comments on what he does and learns. Scrapbooks can hold photos, postcards, souvenirs and brochures from field trips, travel, and special projects. Journals and diaries can be kept by either or both parents along with the homeschooler.

Reading lists. Students keep lists of the books they read, the audiotapes they hear, and the videos they watch.

Portfolio of work. Some parents include a certified teacher's evaluation of the portfolio, which may include:

- ◆ writings—essays, poems, letters, short stories, speeches, Web design and text
- ◆ certificates and awards
- ◆ photojournalism
- ◆ drawings
- ◆ audio/video tapes and photographs of projects
- ◆ mentor comments

Self evaluations: Many gifted students are quite able to evaluate their own effort, progress, and resulting work. Be careful, however, that your child isn't too self-critical. Perfectionism will be discussed in Chapter 4. Compare and discuss with your child your assessments and his assessments in three areas:

- ◆ effort put into the project
- ◆ mastery of the material
- ◆ the finished project

▶ RUBRICS AND EXAMPLES

A **rubric**, or *scoring chart*, is used to evaluate writing samples. Typically, it is a grid that lists the levels of achievement, such as content, development, organization, and conventions, as well as the varying degrees of quality within those categories. "Grades" are usually a range of numbers—for example, 0–4, a score of 4 being the highest.

The following chart is a rubric your family can use to analyze writing, from short answers to short stories. (Note: You may apply the same evaluative standards to a verbal response as you do to a written one.) Don't let these categories intimidate you; the rubric is just a tool. There are other rubrics in Appendix A, where you will find answer keys and samples to the problems found at the end of each chapter.

A variety of writing examples will be displayed within the chapters and in Appendix A.

Category	Knowledge and Understanding	Organization	Use of Support Material	Sentence Structure	Vocabulary	Grammar
Description:	The writing exhibits understanding and interpretation of the task.	The writing develops ideas with a coherent, logical, and orderly approach.	The writing exhibits use of relevant and accurate examples to support ideas.	The writing uses varied sentence structure.	The writing uses effective language and challenging vocabulary.	The writing uses conventional spelling, punctuation, paragraphing, capitalization, grammar, and usage.
4	Your child has a good understanding of the topic and writes about it in an imaginative and creative way.	Your child has organized and developed his/her ideas in a coherent and well-defined manner.	Your child purposely uses support material that is relevant and appropriate.	Your child shows the ability to vary sentence structure.	Your child uses sophisticated vocabulary.	Your child makes few mechanical errors, if any.
3	Your child shows an understanding of the topic and writes about it in a logical, practical way.	Your child had an obvious plan to develop his/her ideas that was satisfactory.	Your child has used some support material in an organized form.	Your child has used correct sentence structure, but there is little sentence variety.	Your child shows an average range of vocabulary.	Your child makes some mechanical errors, but they do not interfere with communication.
2	Your child tries to develop the topic, but digresses and writes about other topics as well.	Your child shows little organization and development of content.	Your child does not use relevant support material.	Your child shows some knowledge of sentence structure, but also writes in fragments or run-on sentences.	Your child uses inaccurate, inexact, or vague language.	Your child makes many mechanical errors that interfere with communication.
1	Your child only addresses the topic minimally.	Your child shows no ability to organize or develop ideas.	Your child has not included or organized support material.	Your child does not have a sense of structure.	Your child uses inexact or immature language.	Your child makes mechanical errors that make the paper impossible to understand.
0	A ZERO paper would be one that shows no relation to the topic, is illegible, incoherent, or blank.	A ZERO paper would be one that shows no relation to the topic, is illegible, incoherent, or blank.	A ZERO paper would be one that shows no relation to the topic, is illegible, incoherent, or blank.	A ZERO paper would be one that shows no relation to the topic, is illegible, incoherent, or blank.	A ZERO paper would be one that shows no relation to the topic, is illegible, incoherent, or blank.	A ZERO paper would be one that shows no relation to the topic, is illegible, incoherent, or blank.

This scoring rubric has been adapted from the New York State standards.

▶ INFINITE RESOURCES

Your bright middle schooler may already be well versed in drawing upon the vast wealth of resources available for inspiration and research. These include:

Print resources: books, newspapers, magazines, photos, plays, essays, graphics, recipes, and poetry

Electronic resources: TV, video, radio, audiocassettes, DVDs, and CD-ROMs

Cyber resources: websites, search engines, e-mail, and software programs

Human resources: oral history, interviews, folk tales, songs, speeches, and epic poems—told by relatives, friends, mentors, reference librarians, elders, and peers

Physical resources: nature, sports, games, and manipulatives

Performing and fine arts: works of music, voice, film, dance, theater, photography, painting, sculpture, crafts, and architecture

Now let's take a look at each of the basic language arts skills—reading, writing, listening, and speaking—that will be addressed in the next four chapters, starting with reading.

▶ THE BASIC SKILLS: READING

Arthur was a so-called "late" reader, but now he devours books on Civil War history and science fantasy. Shy gifted children may also be very eager readers. Reading is often referred to as a key to freedom—the person who masters and enjoys reading will have adventures and friends and discoveries as close as the nearest bookstore or library. Studies show that reading aloud to your children and having reading materials around the house are the two best indicators of future avid readers.

The general goals for reading, at any skill level and any age, are these:

1. To read with understanding and fluency
2. To read and relate to literature representing diverse societies, eras, and ideas
3. To read for the enjoyment of it

THE BASIC SKILLS: WRITING

Jarrod writes a gracious invitation to his next-door neighbor. Carla knows how to turn her choir's monthly meeting notes into clear, concise, and accurate minutes. Matt keeps a journal of his thoughts and poetry. How will these skills translate into future success for Jarrod, Carla, and Matt?

Clear writing is critical to future schooling and employment in today's world. Individuals must be capable of writing for a variety of audiences in differing styles, including standard rhetoric themes, business letters and reports, financial proposals, e-mails, and technical and professional communications. Students should also be able to use computers to enhance their writing proficiency and improve career opportunities, as well as for writing pleasure.

The general goals for writing, at any skill level and any age, are these:

1. To write to communicate or inform
2. To write to convince or encourage action
3. To write for expression, for the enjoyment of it, even for yourself alone

The Three Kinds of Writing

Some gifted children excel in written communication at a young age and some "lag behind" their age peers. At an online chat room for gifted youth, Winona's writing is careless and wordy, but full of ideas, while Charles's writing is succinct and exact. Writing is a most important life skill, as well as a potential source of satisfaction. Teaching writing takes practice and more practice: There are many fine websites and manuals to guide you in teaching your homeschooler.

While they can be interwoven, the three basic kinds of writing are informative, narrative, and persuasive.

Informative writing communicates information to the reader, to share knowledge or to convey messages, instructions, and ideas. Informative writing encompasses reports, letters, e-mails, memos, speeches, and articles. An informative writing exercise would be to write directions to the gym.

Persuasive writing seeks to convince the reader or influence her to take some action. It often contains factual information, such as reasons, examples, or comparisons. However, its main purpose is not to inform, but to persuade. Examples of persuasive writing might be letters to the editor, a restaurant review, or taking sides in a debate. A persuasive writing exercise would be to support this statement: "More bike paths near the park should be paid for by the city."

Narrative writing produces stories, poems, journals, lyrics, or plays. Narrative writers exercise their powers of observation and creativity to poetry or prose that can capture a reader's imagination. A narrative writing exercise might call for finishing a story.

▶ THE BASIC SKILLS: SPEAKING AND LISTENING

Of all the language arts, listening and speaking are those most often used day in and out. Skill in speaking is universally recognized as a primary indicator of a person's knowledge, competence, and credibility. Gifted young people often have the vocabulary and speech patterns of educated adults. The down side of this is that some people assume that an articulate child is gifted across the board, in all areas, or is emotionally and socially mature—which may not be the case.

In person, by phone, or through video, good listening and speaking skills are essential to sending, receiving, and understanding messages. To understand messages and meanings spoken by others, we should listen sensitively—a skill for everyone to work on. In speaking properly and getting our messages across, grammar, sentence structure, tone, expression, and emphasis are parts of the repertoire.

Why do we listen and speak? For basically the same reasons we read and write—to pass information back and forth and partake in narration, creativity, and persuasion. The general goals for speaking and listening, at any skill level and any age, are:

1. To speak clearly and correctly—using appropriate vocabulary, grammar, tone, expression and usage—in a variety of situations

2. To listen attentively, clarifying that you have heard correctly

3. To develop a critical ear—being able to understand what has been said and what has been omitted

▶ RESEARCH, REVISING, AND EDITING

Good reading, writing, speaking, and listening may also entail research, revising, and editing to reach a level of mastery that we would be proud for our gifted middle schooler to attain.

Research
Gifted students are usually no strangers to research because they love to ask questions and absorb knowledge. Bernice and her brother, for example, look up major league baseball statistics before a home game.

Be sure you encourage research of a wide spectrum: written, visual, oral, and electronic. Many homeschoolers know that conducting research can be fun, including:

◆ identifying what questions to ask
◆ hunting for clues and answers
◆ locating sources (library, Internet, video, CD-ROMs, living experts)
◆ selecting and organizing details
◆ separating bias from fact
◆ determining the accuracy and reliability of materials or sources
◆ writing or speaking based on acquired information

Just as research is a pre-writing skill, revising and editing (or proofreading) are skills that come into play after the writing has begun.

Revising and Editing (Plus Proofreading)
Revising and editing are the two last steps of writing that often get "left out." Trey's dad finally convinced him that his highly creative proposal for a science fair project might not be accepted by the review board if Trey didn't clean up his spelling and punctuation. Also, couldn't that last paragraph be worded more clearly? Trey's dad is right. It may seen tedious to a quick thinker, but mistakes in

grammar, usage, punctuation, spelling, and clarity color a reader's perception of the work—no matter how fine the research or thought process is.

Revising involves taking a first, or rough, draft and "tightening" it:

- improving the organization
- sharpening the focus
- clarifying fuzzy logic
- unifying tone
- adding detail and example
- refining vocabulary
- eliminating extraneous material or ideas
- proofreading for errors in vocabulary, grammar, punctuation, and usage

Editing, as well as proofreading, is best begun following a break from writing. Your bright learner will be better able to concentrate and conserve energy. When editing, look for specific errors, not the general meaning. Editing is not a substitute for, but a supplement to, reading for meaning. Clever students will experiment with various editing and proofreading strategies, like these:

- Cover your writing with a piece of paper and work your way down, line by line.
- Read your writing aloud or ask someone to read it to you, in order to *hear* mistakes.
- Proofread backward for spelling and spacing errors.
- Use a spellchecker when writing on a computer, but also reread, as spellcheckers miss usage errors.
- Identify typical errors (for example, problems with subject/verb agreement).
- Look for your own personal, recurring mistakes, such as misspelling "separate."
- Try to understand why you made errors (were you rushed, tired, hungry?).
- Develop a plan to learn the rule and correction for each error.
- Get a parent or friend to read your writing and make constructive comments.

Revising, editing, and proofreading take lots of practice and require the development of good habits. The best thing you can do is to revise, edit, and proofread *with* your homeschooler, so he or she can ask questions and make immediate repairs.

GIFTED KIDS LOVE WORD FUN

What is "Madam, I'm Adam" spelled backward? "Madam, I'm Adam!" That's called a palindrome. A common trait of gifted learners is enjoying word play, such as these examples:

Palindrome = a word or phrase spelled the same forward and backward. *Hannah; Dee saw a seed.*

Anagram = A word or phrase formed by reordering the letters of another word or phrase, such as *satin* to *stain.* Some people make anagrams out of names; for example, author Craig Thomas becomes "got charisma."

Pun = A play on words that sound alike: *Cantaloupe tonight, the ladder's too short!*

Portmanteau word = A new word made by combining two others. *Smog = smoke + fog.*

Lexigram = A word or phrase made up from the letters in another word and defining it. *Titanic = a tin can.*

Etymology = A word's or expression's derivation and history. *The mermaid enthralled the sailor. Thrall is Anglo Saxon for "slave." When you enthrall someone, you reduce him to the condition of a thrall, or you "enslave" him.*

Malapropism = A misused word or phrase: *I just saw a plain-clothes police car!*

Antonym = A word that means the opposite of the first. *The antonym of angelic is devilish.*

Synonym = A word that means the same as the first. *Synonyms of red are crimson and scarlet.*

Tom Swiftie = A sentence ending in "Tom said [rule]" with an adverbial play on words. *"I've got a flat!" Tom said tirelessly,* or *"That door frame is too low," Tom said archly.*

Daffynition = A silly definition made with a real word in the wrong place: *The two doctors are a paradox.*

Onomatopoeia = A word that sounds like what it describes. Examples: *sizzle, pop.*

Acronym = A word spelled with the first letter or letters of several words. *NOW = National Organization for Women* or *WHO = World Health Organization.*

Novel Definition = A real word with a clever new definition. *Coffee (n.), a person who is coughed upon,* or *Eyedropper (n.) A clumsy ophthalmologist.*

The Washington Post Invitational = Any word altered by adding, subtracting, or changing ONE letter and supplying a new definition. *Giraffiti: Vandalism spray-painted very, very high* or *Dopeler effect: The tendency of stupid ideas to seem smarter when they come at you rapidly.*

▶ THE EMOTIONAL WELL-BEING OF YOUR BRIGHT CHILD

Being smart has a lot of pressure attached to it—both external and internal pressures—to succeed and excel. Dr. Deborah Ruf, an educator for the gifted, has some great tips for the emotional well being of gifted families:

1. ***DO provide intellectual challenges.*** Enrich your bright child's education, but look out for perfectionism, test anxiety, and fear of failure.
2. ***DON'T over-schedule.*** Give your learner the freedom to make relaxation choices and down-time to process ideas, read for fun, and just vegetate.
3. ***DON'T focus the challenge*** on either your child's strengths or weaknesses. Allow her to pursue her highest interests and abilities.
4. ***DO help him to recognize*** which skills and knowledge will be important for any normally functioning adult citizen, such as clear writing, filling out forms, and basic math.
5. ***DO give compliments*** to your student for her abilities and efforts; gifted people need recognition from those who matter most.

6. **DON'T hold your child up as an example** for siblings or other children to emulate, compete with, or follow. Comparisons can make a gifted child tone down his gifts so as not to feel freakish, they also put other children in an unfair position.

7. **DO demonstrate how to prioritize**, schedule, and let go. Sometimes gifted kids get over-scheduled and over-involved and they can't decide how to lower their stress and commitments. Help them learn how to pick and choose how they use their time and how to prioritize goals.

8. **DON'T worry that helping your gifted child know** herself better will lead to a "big head" or know-it-all attitude. The more intelligent a person is, the more likely she is to know what she *doesn't* know yet.

9. **DO enjoy this wonderful time in your life.** Have fun with this person you are homeschooling. Enjoy one of the hallmarks of giftedness—a well-developed sense of humor. And take time to appreciate what a gift you are to each other.

▶ HOW THE NEXT FOUR CHAPTERS WILL UNFOLD

The next four chapters are divided into highlighted goals and methods that are generally recognized by parents of gifted homeschoolers as important for a student's mastery of language arts. Each of the next four chapters:

- ◆ details one language arts goal
- ◆ addresses one or more techniques for teaching gifted learners
- ◆ explores how to gauge progress and success
- ◆ provides a sample problem set with answers and explanations
- ◆ discusses how to teach and practice skills involved
- ◆ offers many fun and appropriate activities for all levels of mastery and for all learning styles
- ◆ presents practice sets of different skill levels, with keys and sample answers in Appendix A

Each chapter addresses reading, writing, listening, speaking, research, revising, editing, proofreading, and other competencies, for a particular goal:

- ◆ Social Interaction
- ◆ Information and Understanding
- ◆ Critical Analysis
- ◆ Literary Response and Expression

Each chapter also introduces a specific highlighted method especially adapted for gifted learners. Once again, you will want to adapt and adjust these techniques to fit your particular bright and unique child.

Since children exhibit a range of mastery throughout the middle school years, three levels of challenge are offered in many of our exercises, Levels 1 through 3. In addition, the learning styles discussed on pages 4–5 will be referred to when possible.

CHAPTER 2: *Social Interaction*

Highlighted Goal: **Language Arts for Social Interaction** *Learners read, write, listen, and speak for social interaction.* Students use oral and written language that follows the conventions of the English language with a wide variety of people. As readers and listeners, they use the social communications of others to enrich their understanding of people and their views.

Highlighted Method: **Self-directed Learning, Self-generated Results** *Many gifted students learn best with self-directed learning and/or self-generated projects.* Learners are offered meaningful learning choices and resources to follow their interests or goals. Contracts and project work are explored.

CHAPTER 3: *Information and Understanding*

Highlighted Goal: **Language Arts for Information and Understanding** *Learners read, write, listen, and speak for information and understanding.* As listeners and readers, students collect data and ideas; discover relationships and generalizations; and use knowledge generated from oral, written, and electronic texts. As speakers and writers, learners use oral and written language to acquire, interpret, apply, and transmit information.

Highlighted Method: **Total Immersion and Unit Studies** *Many gifted students prefer total immersion in the subject they are studying.* Learners find that this characteristic lends itself to both in-depth and unit studies.

CHAPTER 4: *Critical Analysis and Evaluation*

Highlighted Goal: **Language Arts for Critical Analysis and Evaluation** *Learners read, write, listen, and speak for critical analysis.* As listeners and readers, gifted students analyze experiences, ideas, information, and issues presented by others. As speakers and writers, they use oral and written language to give opinions on experiences, ideas, information, and issues.

Highlighted Method: **Using Higher Level Thinking Skills** *Many gifted students use higher level thinking than their age peers.* Learners may excel at such activities as brainstorming, problem solving, association, and analysis.

CHAPTER 5: *Literary Response and Expression*

Highlighted Goal: **Language Arts for Literary Response and Expression** *Learners read, write, listen, and speak for literary response and expression.* Gifted students read and listen to oral, written, and electronic texts and performances from American and world literature, relating these to their own lives; they develop an understanding of diverse social, historical, and cultural dimensions. As speakers and writers, learners use oral and written language for self-expression and artistic creation.

Highlighted Method: **The Creative Process** *Many gifted learners excel at using creative processes.* Many gifted homeschoolers experience creativity through a more organic (inborn) than cognitive (learned) path.

For further language arts terms and definitions, please visit the language arts glossary of terms in Appendix B.

Reading, Writing, Listening, and Speaking for Social Interaction

GOAL: *Learners read, write, listen, and speak for social interaction.* Students use oral and written language that follows the conventions of the English language with a wide variety of people. As readers and listeners, they use the social communications of others to enrich their understanding of people and their views.

METHOD: *Many gifted students learn best with self-directed learning and/or self-generated products.* Learners are offered meaningful learning choices and resources to follow their interests or goals. Contracts and project work are explored.

Fresh from the airport, Nora's mother turned onto their street. As she listened to her 13-year-old recount her stay with friends, Claire wondered if Nora would notice that nine diseased trees had been removed from their street. After all, Nora seldom noticed her surroundings. Later, however, Claire found Nora contemplating one new hole after another. Then Nora asked a storm of questions: What disease attacked the trees? How can someone save a diseased tree?

"I don't know," Claire replied. "Why don't you find out?"

Nora threw herself into researching trees and their diseases. Claire knew Nora was capable of great concentration, but she was surprised when Nora missed her favorite television show to spend more time reading about diseased trees. Claire could sense that Nora wanted to do something constructive with her new knowledge but was stymied about what to do.

So Claire did her own research. She discovered a group that contributed money to local environmental causes. "Why don't you create a presentation?" Claire suggested to Nora. "Ask them to help you save trees. The group meets next week."

▶ LANGUAGE ARTS FOR SOCIAL INTERACTION— WHAT DO WE MEAN?

If Nora does indeed address the group next week, she will be speaking to and listening to her audience, trying to persuade them to take action to save local trees. She will have read and written about trees and their diseases, perhaps interviewing experts and discussing her research with her family. Nora is practicing language arts skills for *social interaction*.

Social interaction means participating in our culture. We, as parents, want our children to participate in the satisfying exchange of ideas and feelings. We also know that job requirements often demand "excellent communication skills."

General Activities for Social Interaction

Activities appropriate to Social Interaction goals for your gifted learner include:

- ◆ *Reading* personal letters, e-mails, cards, notes, postcards, electronic discussions, instructions, directions, and invitations
- ◆ *Writing* letters, e-mails, cards, thank-you notes, postcards, instructions, directions, invitations, opinions, and personal essays
- ◆ *Listening* to conversation, group discussions, personal reviews, speeches, directions, foreign languages, and meetings
- ◆ *Speaking* to give instructions, directions, messages, opinions, greetings, introductions, announcements, and for conversation, group discussion, foreign language, interviewing, presentations, and conducting a meeting

What Skills Are We Looking For?

We are guiding our middle schoolers to eventually master and excel in these language arts skills:

- ◆ Using written and spoken messages to establish and enhance personal relationships (*Tracy writes to Aunt Paula, asking to work in her office for one week.*)
- ◆ Writing/reading cards, notes, letters, and e-mails to/from friends, relatives, and neighbors (*Drew exchanges e-mails with friends from his nature walk group.*)
- ◆ Speaking to deliver messages, greetings, and introductions (*Stella introduces her youth group friends to her great-uncle.*)
- ◆ Developing a personal understanding and perspective of what is read and heard (*Molly presents her impressions of a Discovery Channel show on polar bears that she viewed.*)
- ◆ Listening for details and both verbal and non-verbal cues (*Rex listens to and directs a lost child at the zoo.*)
- ◆ Giving and writing instructions and directions (read more in Chapter 3) (*Louise explains how to adjust a carburetor, a lesson she learned from watching her older brother Hank in the driveway last week.*)

- Writing formal letters to inform or persuade (read more in Chapters 3 and 4) *(Joey writes a letter to his congressperson explaining why he thinks there should be more national wildlife preserves.)*
- Revising and editing for correct spelling, grammar, punctuation, and usage *(Darren helps his brother revise and edit a newsletter article on skateboard parks.)*
- Being comfortable in informal conversation *(At his family reunion, Zane learns that his cousin likes chess as much as he does.)*

▶ EVIDENCE OF GROWTH IN GIFTED LEARNERS

You might ask, "What shows progress in my gifted child's work from year to year?" and "How do I evaluate growth regarding repetition of the same activity, such as writing a personal letter?"

What works well is to consider progress in light of the five categories *range, flexibility, connections, conventions,* and *independence.* As a matter of fact, you can assess progress in these five categories with *any* language arts standard or goal:

1. *Range*—breadth and depth of topics, issues, treatments (often a prominent gifted characteristic)
2. *Flexibility*—performance in changing and varied conditions
3. *Connections*—ability to see similarities and bridge themes (often a prominent gifted characteristic)
4. *Conventions*—rules, protocols, traditional practices in English
5. *Independence*—ability to perform without direction (often a prominent gifted characteristic)

For the materials covered in this chapter, *social interaction goals,* ask yourself, "Over the years, does my gifted learner show progress in:

1. writing and talking to a diverse **range** of individuals and groups? in a diverse **range** of topics? giving verbal and non-verbal signals?
2. adapting with more **flexibility** to people of different ages, genders, cultural groups, and social positions? with more **flexibility** in assuming appropriate roles in conversation?
3. making stronger **connections** with the interests, experiences, and feelings of another person or group?
4. understanding more deeply the **conventions** of behavior, of tone and diction, and of verbal and non-verbal language?
5. initiating conversations with a greater **independence**? adapting language and personal role to the listener/reader?"

▶ EVIDENCE OF SUCCESS IN SOCIAL INTERACTION

Many families with gifted children resist grade-specific measurement of their children's success, such as "Kira reads at a seventh-grade level." These labels can be fairly meaningless when attached to a gifted learner, who may be difficult to test or may have very divergent abilities. For example, Miguel tested several years ahead of his peers in math and associative reasoning, but was a "late" reader—what grade level do you assign Miguel for either math or reading?

Luckily, one of the advantages of homeschooling a gifted child is freeing her to work at her own pace, in her own learning style(s), and not having to master any one subject by a specified time, nor to absorb all subjects to the same degree at a certain age.

You know your middle schooler's proficiency and progress best. With your help, your middle schooler will move into mastery of language arts skills at his own rate, in his own best manner. So, how will you recognize mastery in reading, writing, listening, and speaking for social interaction? Consider these accomplishments.

EXAMPLES OF MASTERY *include*

- writing letters to local and distant friends
- sharing how he or she feels about a letter or journal entry
- initiating a conversation with a senior citizen at the dentist's office
- beginning to adjust vocabulary and style to match a reader or listener
- using a variety of print and electronic forms for social communication with peers and adults
- sending/receiving e-mail messages on a computer network
- exploring communication with members of other groups and cultures
- sending formal invitations to family parties or open houses
- participating in family and small group discussions
- giving announcements or a short speech at a party
- listening to others and building upon their comments in turn
- learning some words in another language and using them with speakers of that language

EXAMPLES OF ADVANCED MASTERY *include further development of the above and*

- writing personal notes and letters to entertain and interest the reader
- adjusting vocabulary and style to account for the nature of a relationship and the interests and needs of the reader
- communicating to some degree in another language
- responding to a newspaper story with an opinion letter
- reading and completing part-time job applications
- communicating effectively with members of other groups and cultures
- participating in electronic discussion groups
- participating in and conducting a meeting
- interacting with community members through community service or part-time jobs

- writing letters and personal essays as part of a practice college application or summer program
- interviewing for a job or college class

Now let's examine a writing assignment and three sample responses. Your student may, of course, practice with any of the exercises in this book. Throughout *Homeschooling Your Gifted Child: Language Arts for the Middle School Years*, you will find examples of three levels of mastery.

▶ SAMPLE EXERCISE

Write an *acknowledgment* (a public thank you), thanking a mentor for helping you complete a project or another goal. (*Note:* Student may write one to four paragraphs, depending on level of proficiency. This exercise extends social interaction skills from an oral "thank you" to a third-person acknowledgement.)

_____
_____
_____
_____
_____
_____
_____
_____
_____
_____
_____

Examples and Comments

The following are three examples of successful answers to the short essay prompt above, along with some comments to help you evaluate your learner's writing. Essay grading is, of course, somewhat subjective, so we are providing the reasoning supporting Levels 1, 2, and 3. Nevertheless, you have the right to disagree!

Level 1 Example

I would like to thank my mentor, Mr. Morey, for helping me make a hardwood stand for my mom's Shona sculpture. It turned out amazing. He also taught me how to sand and varnish the stand at home. Thanks, too, belong to Mrs. Morey, who prompted Mr. Morey to have me wear goggles and gloves near the saw and drill!

Writer answers the prompt in an acceptable way; reflects understanding of a simple genre, the acknowledgement; manipulates the basic conventions of spelling, punctuation, capitalization, and usage correctly. Some nice use of vocabulary ("Thanks, too, belong to . . ." and "prompted"). Shows wit—a very common characteristic of gifted children.

Level 2 Example

Wow, I won second place in the Hawthorne Homeschoolers Science Fair! This hard–earned honor came to my science project entitled "Potential and Kinetic Energy in Rubber Bands." I couldn't have accomplished this without my father, who took the time to help me with the posters and those annoying tables in *Excel*. He is certainly a great inspiration to me. I want to thank him for his time, patience, and efforts extended to make my project look great.

Thanks, Dad, for all your help and love. I could not have won without you. Even though I did tell you I thought I could, I couldn't. And I'm here to tell you "thank you" right now.

(In addition to the comments given previously) Writer successfully combines formal and colloquial language ("efforts extended," and "I would like to thank," and "thanks, Dad,"), recognizing the dual audiences for the text: a general audience and a specific person; shows an appreciation of social interaction customs; provides detail (project title) and example ("the posters and those annoying tables in Excel*").*

Level 3 Example

Imagine a friend so awesome and accomplished that you crave her company. You long to watch her at her work and to debate with her and to share her wisdom. Imagine a teacher who also loves being a student. She respects you and makes you laugh. You have now imagined my mentor, Lisa Bartlett!

Lisa has taught me everything I know (so far) about horses. She loaned me her single-lens reflex (SLR) camera to take pictures of Champ and Buddy. She let me practice developing black-and-white pictures in her studio darkroom. Lisa also inspired me to read *My Friend Flicka* and *Thunderhead*, two excellent novels by Mary O'Hara, and to watch some great horsy films like *National Velvet* and *The Black Stallion*. In addition, Lisa taught me many important things about the raising and care of horses.

I devised a way to compile all this information and photos and some of my sketches in a gigantic scrapbook and journal. I did most of this work by myself, but I nevertheless need to thank Lisa, because without her teaching me to love and respect these four-legged marvels, I wouldn't have the information and skills I have today.

I did well on my scrapbook precisely because my mentor motivates me. Finally, she is kind enough to help me out with my terrible spelling. Imagine someone like that and you have Lisa Bartlett in mind.

(In addition to the comments given above) Writer adds empathy and humor; uses advanced syntax and vocabulary; uses personal references to reinforce the nature of the relationship between the writer and the person being thanked; adds detail and example to teach the reader ["single-lens reflex (SLR)"]; uses correct paragraphing and complex sentences; wraps up the assignment with a nod to the introductory paragraph.

► SELF-DIRECTED LEARNING, SELF-GENERATED RESULTS

What Is Self-Directed Learning?

Gifted kids are commonly strongly motivated to do things that interest them (but in their own way). Some love to work independently; some with a mentor who accepts original thought. Gifted learners want to make discoveries and solve problems. They often have several passionate interests, collections, or hobbies. In short, they are good candidates for self-directed learning. What does that mean?

1. **Self-directed learning can mean working on your own.** Many gifted children are very independent and can focus to the point of becoming "lost" in their work or play. Take Jonah, who read *Ender's Game*—Orson Scott Card's science fiction novel about gifted children—one evening for five straight hours. His parents gladly let him because Jonah had been a so-called "late" reader and now appeared to be making up for it!

2. **Self-directed learning can mean having a vested interest in what you are working on.** All children, but gifted children in particular, need to be allowed to explore areas of passion to them. Look at Rachel, who has always loved dinosaurs and is now building a stegosaurus skeleton and attending an archeological dig at the La Brea Tar Pits.

3. **Self-directed evaluation can be worthwhile.** Gifted students tend to be able to recognize their own strengths and weaknesses. Note that James decided to practice with his Spanish software for an extra half-hour because he knows he has difficulty remembering verb forms.

In order to follow self-directed interests and goals, learners need parents who will

- help them select safe and meaningful learning choices
- suggest resources
- provide resources when needed
- teach time management
- guide in goal-setting and self-evaluation
- help keep the learner on-task and teach skills for keeping on-task

Self-Generated Results

A common trait of gifted learners is rebelling against routine and predictability and resisting taking orders. Sound familiar? Well, if it does, congratulations—homeschooling is ideal for gifted kids because they usually have more freedom to produce their own results (or products) from their learning experiences. These results usually take the form of one of the following:

- exhibitions
- reports
- performances
- written, video, or audio products
- projects

Projects

The following challenging project ideas are meant to take language arts across the curriculum.

- Create a magazine or newsletter, maybe on a specific theme.

- Trace the genealogy of your family and design a family tree, a history album, or a family crest.

- Design the perfect broom, car, stove, etc.

- Keep a nature journal.

- Create a booklet evaluating all the parks in your town (rate play equipment, playing fields, restrooms, gardens).

- Keep a family journal, where everyone contributes writings and drawings.

- Maintain a diary of your thoughts, feelings, hopes, and dreams for one month.

- Build a castle or bridge from your own plans.

- Invent a board game. Make the board. Invent a card game and teach it to someone else.

- Organize a neighborhood Science Fair.

- Design your own language or code.

- Invent a sport, complete with logical rules, equipment, and uniforms.

- Research a subject you love at the library and online, in all kinds of media.

- Interview an older person, a veteran, or your mentor on tape or video.

TAKE THE CHALLENGE!

A diary is one very intimate way to express yourself. Sometimes sharing a journal or diary can deeply affect others. For example, *The Diary of Anne Frank,* written by gifted creative thinker Anne Frank when she was 13 and 14 years old, has been translated into 67 languages! It is one of the most beloved books in the world.

Here is a list of websites and fan sites about Anne, many displaying rare family photos. Explore these sites. Read Anne's own words in her diary.

Compare the diary to the film, TV movie, or documentaries about Anne. Investigate other published diaries. Keep your own diary for a month.

Anne Frank: Her Life and Times: A Scrapbook
   www.annefrank.com/site/af_life/2_life_scrp/2_life_scrapbook.htm
St. Petersburg Times' Newspaper in Education (a series of excellent articles that are printable called
Anne Frank: Lessons in Human Rights and Dignity)
   www.sptimes.com/nie/nieanne.html
An amazing cutaway view of the Anne Frank House and attic (especially interesting after viewing the movie)
   members.aol.com/macbloom/Pages/techill.html#AnchorAFMuseum

Rare photos of Anne and her family
    www.e-lysian.com/jayse/annefrank/photos.htm
Photos of Anne's actual diary, pen, and desk
    www.e-lysian.com/jayse/annefrank/diary.htm
The opened diary with photos of Anne in it
    www.gurlpages.com/juliefoudy/Annefrank.html
Photos of where the Franks lived before they went into hiding and their schools, including the one
with Anne's diary on the outside walls
    www.nicole-caspari.de/annefrank/e_pictures.html
Resource page for Anne Frank
    www.angelfire.com/journal2/afdiary/recomnd.htm

Questions to Pursue:
- Why do you think Anne Frank and her writings are so loved?
- What themes and feelings are universal in Anne's writing?
- How do you compare Anne's diary to the works *about* her?
- What areas of history are you led to pursue?
- What do you like/dislike about the diary/journal format?
- What other diaries and journals are well known in literature or history?

Process or Product?

Some gifted children abandon projects without finishing them. To them, the "finish what you start" rule feels unreasonable. This learner may steadfastly follow some projects for days or weeks, through completion, while deserting others shortly after beginning them. This can be very frustrating for a parent, but the truth is, this child may have already learned all she needed or wanted to know. Or she may have found another, more fascinating, path. Or she may have decided the project wasn't worth her time. A gifted child is likely to value *process* more than *product*.

Some parents may feel that letting a child drop a project discourages self-discipline. Another view, by Stephanie Tolan, in her essay "Stuck in Another Dimension," suggests that "it isn't letting them avoid normal school tasks that diminishes self-discipline, but forcing them to do all tasks, including those inappropriate to their capabilities." Tolan says *boredom* is the killer of discipline.

As for producing a product, most of us are product oriented. How can we prove we have learned skills if we don't have a paper or a report or a project to show for it? A successful product illustrates an understanding of content and process. Often we think of results in terms of written work. OK, but maybe we should look at alternatives to written work for our gifted children.

In fact, some gifted learners resist written products because their brains move much faster than their hands can type or write. They may, however, be enthusiastic about "real-life products for appropriate audiences," such as a play or an exhibition or a portfolio or a piano concert. You might want to discuss this issue with your homeschooler to see where you both stand.

Whatever your choice, whether producing a product, working on a single project or an entire subject area, some homeschoolers prefer setting down their goals in a learning contract, or study agreement: Keesha feels it keeps her on track; Frank likes to see his goals in writing; and Carlos likes to show his parents his progress on a timeline. Parents usually appreciate that a contract takes responsibility off of their shoulders and places it onto the learner's.

Learning Contracts

A learning contract best serves its purpose if it has built-in flexibility, for example, if a deadline needs to be moved or a new avenue of exploration appears and changes the course of the project. In other words, the contract may be revised and adjusted as necessary, in good faith, as long as the learner and the parent agree.

Here is one sample contract:

SAMPLE LEARNING CONTRACT

(Note: There are many, many formats for learning contracts, both in books and online.)

Name: *Lisa Pallay*   **STARTING DATE:** *January 12*   **GOAL DATE:** *February 12*

TOPIC I WANT TO INVESTIGATE: *Maya Angelou*

I.   QUESTIONS TO ANSWER:

1. Why does Angelou write about what she writes about?

2. What are some of her experiences?

3. At which inauguration did she read "On the Pulse of the Morning"?

4. What makes her poetry so wonderful?

II.   POSSIBLE RESOURCES:

1. *I Know Why the Caged Bird Sings* by Maya Angelou

2. *The Complete Collected Poems* of Maya Angelou

3. Angelou at the Civic Auditorium Speakers Series on January 26 (maybe I can meet her?!)

4. Audiocassettes of Angelou reading her poetry

5. Mini-series *Roots* (she plays Nyo Boto)

6. Fan sites, cyber reviews, and other Internet resources

III.   SHARING WHAT I HAVE LEARNED:

1. Discuss what I have learned.

2. Perform my own reading of my favorite poems of Angelou's.

3. Give a persuasive speech to try to convince my family members or friends to read her books and poetry.

Alternatives:

Design a collage of images from her works.

Write 3 poems on Angelou's themes

IV. EVALUATION

My family and friends will critique my presentations.

_____

{Signed and dated}

How Do You Test or Evaluate Self-Directed Learning?

Some bright students test well, some don't. And conventional tests often just measure the lower-level or basic skills. Therefore, testing self-directed learning will require some imagination on your part, as most tests tend to measure the acquisition of knowledge, rather than the ability to apply the knowledge in various ways.

Rather than testing, you may prefer to evaluate:

- the quality of the work produced
- the innovation of the work produced
- the degree of challenge of the assignment
- the progress of skills being learned
- the wisdom gained from mistakes

As recommended in Chapter 1, gifted students can contribute to the creation of point systems, scoring rubrics, or holistic assessment of their work. (See Appendix A for examples of scoring rubrics.) Responsibility for evaluating work and progress is then shared between parent and learner. A bonus is that self-evaluation is a skill that will continue to benefit any learner through college and life.

▶ TEACHING LISTENING AND SPEAKING SKILLS

Some gifted kids have difficulties with personal communication, with listening, and speaking skills. For example:

- They may sound arrogant or know-it-all.
- They may be shy to speak, in fear of not meeting their own perfectionist standards.
- They may make connections that are difficult for others to understand.
- They may interrupt or be fidgety.
- They may be appear to be daydreaming instead of listening.
- Their brains may be racing ahead of the speaker's words.

Interactions with Ability-Level Peers

Interacting with other people of like intelligence seems to be important to developing your learners social skills. In her article "Appropriate Expectations for the Gifted Child" (www.giftedbooks. com/aart_devries2.html), educator Arlene DeVries tells us, "a peer for a gifted child might be an intellectual peer, an age-level peer, a social or emotional peer, or a physical peer. Because of their wide ranges of abilities and interests, true peers might be found in a number of persons in a variety of age groups. Each individual has a basic need to belong or to be able to relate to someone who is like him- or herself. When children are involved intellectually, emotionally, or artistically with others who think and act as they do, this need is generally met. Self-esteem increases when they are comfortable being their 'real selves' with others who have similar interests, inquiring minds, high energy levels, and a drive to learn. . . . These children need to find places where they can interact with others of like ability, thus increasing their chances of finding 'soul-mates.'"

Here are a few techniques parents can try to help nurture better listening and speaking skills. Feel free to modify the following ideas as you see fit, to continue challenging your learner. Many can evolve into self-generated projects. Some suggestions are further detailed by storyteller/teacher Heather Forest on her website www.storyarts.org.

Listening for Social Interaction

1. Ask your child to write a list of the qualities of a good listener. Read and discuss the list. Probe what your learner doesn't like about listening (being patient? walking in another's shoes?).

2. Assess your own listening skills, learner and parent. Do you always pay complete mental attention to speakers or does your mind stray? What can you do to "bring yourself back"? Brainstorm some ideas.

3. Discuss what a speaker might *really* be feeling or saying "between the lines." Many gifted kids are very empathetic and sensitive to others' feelings. Help develop this sensitivity.

4. Practice showing encouragement to friends or family in non-verbal terms with your eyes, facial expressions, body stance and touching, to show that you are listening. Kinesthetic learners excel at exercises like this one.

Public Speaking

1. Share stories by retelling jokes, folk tales, "shaggy dog stories," or reading a folk tale out loud. While storytelling is often one of the verbal/linguistic learner's strengths, visual learners also enjoy retelling a story after illustrating it.

2. Have your student give an oral book report or act out the parts in a short story, book, or play.

3. Have your learner write and present a first-person monologue, pretending to be someone famous he or she has been studying or saw a film about.

4. Your co-op learning group or family can write a radio show, including family news reports, live interviews, poetry, or headline news.

Share Your Reading with Each Other

What a legacy we leave our children when we pass on a love of reading to them! Parents who fill their homes with books, magazines, and software on a variety of subjects are giving a true gift. Books can be a fantasy world of escape or a stress management tool for your bright, intense learner.

Here are some tips on reading enrichment:

1. Read a short story or book aloud to each other, or choose a book you've both enjoyed reading silently. Award-winning books have already proven themselves worthy of being read. Note: Fantasy or humor are usually easier to listen to than history or biography.

2. Enter the world of the story together, discussing tough issues, sharing how you both feel about the characters, the plot, and the values in the book.

3. Have your learner identify the themes and conflicts in the story. Have your learner compare the characters to those in other readings.

Here are some favorite books from Celine Perillat, age 13, a homeschooled middle schooler.

- *Dealing with Dragons, Searching for Dragons, Calling on Dragons, Talking to Dragons, and The Book of Enchantments* by Patricia C. Wrede
- *Harry Potter* series by J.K. Rowling (I didn't read much before I started to read this series.)
- *The Everworld* series by Katherine A. Applegate
- *The Hobbit* by J.R.R. Tolkien
- *The 7 Habits of Highly Effective Teens* by Sean Covey
- *The Tiger Rising* by Kate DiCamillo

Practicing the Art of Conversation

1. Choose a news event you have read about. Pair up your student with a friend or sibling to discuss, one-on-one, that particular event or issue. Are the kids aware of the necessity of taking turns speaking and listening?

2. Around the table or in the car, make up onomatopoetic words—words that have descriptive sounds. They can be real or make-believe! (Examples: hiss, zap, ding-dong, pop, slither, hush, choo-choo, plunk, click, slarp, smush, screech)

3. Small group members can discuss doing a co-op project, such as a short skit based on a folktale. Kinesthetic and visual learners usually go for acting!

4. Try to sensitize those at the breakfast or dinner table to good listening manners. Mention whenever a speaker is interrupted by others before a communication has been completed. A pause during a speaker's statement may not constitute an opportunity for another person to cut in and speak. Ask the group, "When does a pause allow another person to speak?" "Do we listen more attentively to the tone of a person's voice if we cannot see their facial expressions?"

▶ ACTIVITIES, ACTIVITIES, ACTIVITIES

The following activities have been selected because they are fun and because they enhance the development of social interaction skills. In addition, they are purposeful, practical, and not simply "busy work" or "more of the same" that gifted learners are often handed. Remember, that while *all* students need to develop basic skills, gifted students can often acquire these as they develop their other, more advanced abilities.

Feel free to adapt these activities to your middle schooler's maturity and abilities.

The Autobiography of Anything

Everything has a story! Everything comes, in its elemental origin, from the Earth. First, collect an assortment of "things":

- piece of paper
- sneaker
- match
- rubber band
- paper clip
- woolen socks

Imagine the life story of each of these objects. Describe its history backwards, through your personal use, purchase, manufacture, to original natural resources from which it or its components were made. Personify the thing and tell its story like an autobiography, for example: *Tell the tale of a piece of newspaper back to the tree in the forest*, or *Tell the tale of a plastic toy's life, tracing its history back to the oil that became plastic and then back to the prehistoric plants that created the oil.*

Play "If"

One person in your support group or family gives a hypothetical situation beginning with "If . . . " Each person tries to defend his answer and persuade the others to his viewpoint. (No one is right or wrong.) Sample questions:

1. If you had $10,000,000 to give away, how would you spend it to help the world?
2. If you could eliminate one habit your parent/child/sibling has, what would that be?
3. If you could suddenly possess an extraordinary talent in one of the arts, what would it be?
4. If you could have a free telephone line to any one person in the world, who would it be?
5. If you could add one sentence to the U.S. Constitution, what would it say?

Advice Columnist

Cover up or cut out the answers to questions written to Ann Landers or Dear Abby in one of their newspaper columns. Ask your learner to write or discuss his own replies and then compare them together to the printed replies.

Communication Hunt

Investigate and list ALL forms of communication in your household (from body language to grocery lists to the radio). A pencil doesn't count, but a journal does. Compare lists—who came come up with the most? Who came up with one no one else did? Who can think of forms of communication your household *doesn't* have? (a Star Trek communicator?)

The Jonathan Winters Game

Pick a household item and invent 20 new uses for it, apart from the obvious.

Describing a Stone

Pass a stone around a circle of people. Each person must say one word describing the stone without repeating what has been said. See how many times the stone can go around the circle without repeating words. Adjectives such as *hard, asymmetric,* etc., are a start, but any word that comes to mind is acceptable as long as it is inspired by the stone. For example, a round, white, oval stone could suggest *egg.*

Friendly Persuasion

Write a letter to a member of your family. The letter should try to convince the family member to do something for you or for society. It needs to include reasoning, examples, and details.

Theme Scrabble

Play Scrabble (or any other word game) using only words from a chosen theme, such as farming, holidays, or weather.

Hold a Salon

A *salon* is a conversation party, when an invited group of friends gathers socially to discuss an interesting topic. Hold a salon with other friends, particularly other gifted kids. The first meeting of the salon could be to develop a good list of discussion topics such as ethics, current events, novels or films. Members of the salon may determine the ground rules, such as *respect the diversity of opinions* or *no interrupting.*

Movies Featuring Gifted Kids

It's fun to sit down, watch, and discuss movies together—especially movies featuring gifted children or adults in a positive light. Thanks to www.hoagiesgifted.org, here is a list to get you started:

- *Amazing Grace and Chuck* (rated PG) A 12-year-old Little League whiz decides to stop playing baseball until the world agrees to complete nuclear disarmament. Soon professional athletes follow suit, as his protest escalates.
- *Beauty and the Beast* (animated, rated G) A young woman loves to read and doesn't fit in with the common picture of acceptable society.
- *Billy Elliot* (R) Billy Elliot has problems. He is mourning his mother's death while avoiding his stern father. Billy's working-class dad has scraped together enough money for Billy to have boxing lessons, but Billy has discovered his own aptitude: ballet dancing. He keeps it quiet, until his teacher encourages him to audition for the London Ballet.
- *Contact* (PG) An articulate radio astronomer discovers an alien signal that contains plans for building a transport device to another world.
- *Dead Poets Society* (PG) English professor John Keating inspires his students to love poetry and to seize the day. A compelling warning in this film for parents who don't respect their children's gifts.
- *Empire of the Sun* (PG-13) Twelve-year-old Jim survives on his own wits during the downfall of China in WWII.

- *Finding Forrester* (PG-13) On a dare, Jamal sneaks into Forrester's musty sanctuary, which turns into an inspiring meeting of the minds, with mutual respect and intelligence erasing boundaries of culture and generation
- *Good Will Hunting* (R) A therapist helps a brilliant but troubled young man overcome his personal problems and realize his potential.
- *Infinity* (PG) Early life of Nobel-prize winning physicist Richard Feynman.
- *Little Man Tate* (PG) This little boy is human—not just "a brain." He worries about people dying, envies the popular "jock," and plays music for competition.
- *Matilda* (PG) Comedy based on Roald Dahl's classic book about a bright young girl (in a cretinous family) who learns self-reliance and develops unusual powers.
- *The Mighty* (PG) A presumably dimwitted giant of a seventh-grader and an intelligent-but-diminutive boy combine their best assets to cope with the world.
- *October Sky* (PG) A West Virginia teenager hopes to break free from his predetermined coal miner's life by winning a national science contest with his rocket-building.
- *Searching for Bobby Fischer* (PG) Fascinating tale of the chess prodigy who refuses to become ruthless.
- *Stand and Deliver* (PG) True story of a dedicated teacher who inspires his drop-out class to build self-esteem and learn advanced calculus
- *War Games* (PG) A young man finds a back door into a military central computer in which reality is confused with game-playing

Other films about giftedness: *Angus, The Black Cauldron, Elizabeth, Ferris Bueller's Day Off, Fly Away Home, Gattaca, Harriet the Spy, An Innocent Love, The Iron Giant, Kiki's Delivery Service, The Last Starfighter, Little Buddha, A Little Romance, Ma Vie en Rose, Mr. Holland's Opus, My Left Foot, My Neighbor Totoro, The Power of One, Rain Man, Real Genius, Remember the Titans, Rushmore, Short Circuit, The Secret of Roan Inish, The Tic Code, Willow, Young Einstein*

Summary

Social interaction—an active involvement in our culture—seems to be essential to a human being's happiness and growth. In fact, storyteller-teacher Heather Forest claims that social interaction skills "are essential to participating in adult culture. The ability to articulate thoughts, feelings, and needs can contribute to academic, interpersonal, and professional success. For safety's sake, children need to be able to express their thoughts so they can ask for help and get what they need from adults. And good listeners learn more efficiently."

I. Picturesque Words

Think of synonyms or creative expressions for the following over-used, common, or non-specific words. Use your imagination! After you have come up with as many as you can on your own, ask others for their ideas or look in a thesaurus.

Example:

happy

Some possible answers: joyful, silly, full of beans, joyous, merry, glad, laughy, gleeful, delighted, ecstatic, goofy, jumping on springs, giggly, tickled pink, tickled to death, bubbling over, in seventh heaven, happy as a clam

1. dog

_____

2. red (or shades of)

_____

3. airplane

_____

4. walk (the verb)

_____

5. store (the verb)

_____

6. woman

_____

II. An Object

Note: The answer to this prompt requires social interaction with the reader in explaining one's own feelings, attitude, bias, and experience. An extension to the writing might be reading aloud and then discussing several answers.

Read the following excerpt from a poem by Walt Whitman, from his book *Leaves of Grass* (1891).

There was a child who went forth every day,
And the first object he look'd upon, that
    object he became,
And that object became part of him for
    the day or a certain part of the day,
Or for many years or stretching cycles
    of years.

Whitman's poem suggests that certain objects become important to us and remain important to us even if we no longer have them. Write a story in which you tell about an object that remains important to the main character over a period of years. The main character could be you or someone you know.

In your story, you might describe the main character's first encounter with the object, why the object is so important to the character, and how, over the years, it remains a part of the character's life.

_____
_____
_____
_____
_____
_____
_____
_____
_____
_____
_____
_____
_____
_____
_____
_____
_____
_____
_____
_____
_____
_____
_____
_____
_____
_____
_____
_____
_____
_____

3

Reading, Writing, Listening, and Speaking for Information and Understanding

GOAL: *Learners read, write, listen, and speak for information and understanding. As listeners and readers, students collect data and ideas; discover relationships and generalizations; and use knowledge generated from oral, written, and electronic texts. As speakers and writers, learners use oral and written language to acquire, interpret, apply, and transmit information.*

METHOD: *Many gifted students prefer total immersion in the subject they are studying. Learners find that this characteristic lends itself to in-depth studies and unit studies.*

*T*he *"D" Shawn* received as a first-semester grade from his sixth-grade math teacher, Mr. Martinez, puzzled his parents.

At home Shawn grasped concepts quickly and delighted in using his math skills to solve everyday problems. As a first grader, Shawn already knew how to multiply, although he refused to memorize the multiplication tables. Shawn shrugged off his dad's questions about math class, so Peter, Shawn's dad, met with Mr. Martinez.

"Shawn usually arrives at the right answers," Mr. Martinez said, "but can seldom explain how he reached the answer. And Shawn makes errors that indicate he does not absorb what I am teaching."

Mr. Martinez pulled out a stack of Shawn's recent assignments. "Shawn still doesn't know his multiplication tables."

"Shawn and I have begun exploring basic algebra," Peter said.

"I would recommend that Shawn first learn the remedial skills," Mr. Martinez answered. "I suggest Shawn spend his math time in a fourth-grade class."

"But Shawn already understands basic algebra concepts," Peter replied.

"Shawn is bright," Mr. Martinez agreed. "I just don't see it in his everyday work."

▶ Language Arts for Information and Understanding— What Do We Mean?

Shawn's parents are considering homeschooling him, in the hope that he can pursue his studies and interests in a less-regimented environment. Shawn loves to soak up facts (information) and apply them (understanding), but he definitely has an individual style. For example, in trying to learn and understand the language that is mathematics, Shawn exhibits qualities common to many gifted learners:

- underachieves in a traditional classroom ("D" in math)
- grasps concepts quickly and applies them to everyday life
- lacks interest or is distracted sometimes (shrugs off Peter's questions)
- arrives at an answer without necessarily knowing the process
- is inattentive to detail (makes easy errors)
- has difficulty remembering rote work (multiplication tables)
- displays advanced thinking and reasoning (algebra in sixth grade)

Shawn, his parents, and all of us absorb **information and understanding** from many sources—printed, visual, verbal, and electronic—and it can truly be exhausting work. Add to that the fact that gifted children learn, process, and apply information *differently* than the rest of us, and we have a real challenge to help them.

As parents, we want our children to read well and widely, building a strong foundation for learning in all areas of life. We want them to differentiate between fact and fiction and opinion and bias. In the arenas of schooling and work, we want our learners to be able to research and use a wide variety of resources. These become our goals.

General Activities for Information and Understanding

Activities appropriate to Information and Understanding goals for your gifted learner include

- *Reading* essays, speeches, textbooks, newspapers and magazines, encyclopedias, history, and other fiction and non-fiction text
- *Writing* research reports, essays, lists, outlines, summaries, directions, and instructions
- *Listening* to speeches, fiction and non-fiction excerpts, lectures, documentaries, films, news broadcasts; identifying details and fact, bias and propaganda
- *Speaking* to give speeches, research, instructions, and directions

What Skills Are We Looking For?

We are guiding our gifted middle schoolers to eventually master and excel in these language arts skills:

- Listening and reading to acquire information and understanding (*Eamon paraphrases a documentary on migrant farm workers.*)
- Writing and speaking to teach, explain, or instruct (*Danielle teaches her youth group how to prune the miniature rose bushes.*)
- Asking questions to probe and clarify (*Brendan requests clarification at the town council meeting.*)
- Participating in family discussions (*Brian learns from his dad how to install the printer software and teaches his sister how to change the toner cartridge.*)
- Giving and writing instructions and directions (*Becky tells Steven how to get to her house from the library.*)
- Differentiating fact from bias (*Noi scans an editorial to determine where and how the writer supports his opinions with data.*)
- Applying information from one context to another (*Grace reads instructions for building a small doghouse, then adapts them to design a larger one with two entrances.*)
- Conduct basic research (*At his library, Tomoyuki finds articles, books, and websites to write a report, with pictures, on the Bikini Islands.*)
- Using the computer (*Chantal manipulates the search engine to find a tutorial on making pictographs in* Excel.)
- Revising and editing for correct spelling, grammar, punctuation, and usage (*Ned helps his sister revise and edit the rough draft of a complaint letter to the cellular phone company.*)

▶ EVIDENCE OF SUCCESS IN INFORMATION AND UNDERSTANDING

For a discussion of the five elements of growth in learning—range, flexibility, connections, conventions, and independence—please refer to page 43.

Remember, you know your middle schooler's proficiency and progress best. With your help, your middle schooler will move into mastery of language arts skills at her own rate, in her own best manner. So, how will you recognize mastery of goals for information and understanding? Consider these accomplishments.

EXAMPLES OF MASTERY include

- paraphrasing what has been read or heard and writing summaries
- following directions that involve many steps
- getting clarification of an idea
- revising an early draft of a report to make it clearer
- using facts from news articles and TV reports in an oral report on a current event
- taking notes that record the main ideas and most significant details of a lecture or speech

- writing an essay for science that contains information from interviews, magazines, and the Internet
- participating in a group discussion, citing the sources of information
- using technical terms correctly
- surveying friends or family on an issue and reporting the findings

EXAMPLES OF ADVANCED MASTERY include further development of the above and
- demonstrating how to perform an intricate task
- using an electronic data base to find evidence of trends in society
- producing flow charts or diagrams to show relationships among information
- determining the relative value of different resources
- writing up a science lab report
- producing program notes for an art exhibit or concert with background information on the artists
- producing a science or social studies project or presentation

Now let's examine a writing assignment and three sample responses. Throughout *Homeschooling Your Gifted Child: Language Arts for the Middle School Years*, you will find examples of two to three levels of mastery.

▶ SAMPLE EXERCISE

Research and reply to this question: Who have been the "guests" at the Tower of London?

Examples and Comments
The following are three examples of successful answers to the research question above, along with a rubric to help you evaluate your learner's research and writing.

Level 1 Example
There have been hundreds of "guests" at the Tower of London. If they may be called guests! There were hardly ever any trials involved. There were many escapes and also many terrible executions.

Some of the most famous guests who were executed there were these:

- William Wallace, Scottish rebel leader
- Edward IV's two sons, the two little princes Edward V and Richard, Duke of York
- Sir Thomas More, statesman and loyal friend to Henry VIII
- Anne Boleyn, Henry VIII second wife
- Catherine Howard, Henry VIII fifth wife
- Sir Walter Raleigh, explorer

There were many more people tortured, killed, and buried at the various towers within the Tower of London.

The writer understands the assignment; has shown basic research to answer the question; gives an overall picture; understands the irony of "guest"; cites seven of the famous "guests"; gives brief descriptions of each; mentions that there were several towers; presents a bulleted list; uses correct grammar, word usage, and punctuation.

Level 2 Example

Through the ages, many a frightened person was dragged to the Tower of London and imprisoned. I visited the Tower two years ago and I could easily imagine the moaning and howling that went on there. Some were tortured, some were left to rot for years. Some were in the Tower for imagined sins against their ruler, some for real treacheries.

For example, William Wallace was a Scot rebel leader of Welsh descent who fought many battles against England. He was eventually captured and drawn and quartered—yeach! (Which is what they did in those days.)

Henry VI, usurped by Edward IV, was a real king before he was thrown into prison and executed. But later, Edward IV's two young princes, Edward V and Richard, Duke of York, became famous victims of royal cruelty. People are still very sad about the boys, who used to play in the Tower gardens.

Another celebrated guest was Sir Thomas More, who refused to take an oath and died a hero. Henry VIII's second and fifth wives, Anne and Catherine, both died in the Tower.

And another important one was the explorer Sir Walter Raleigh, who the cigarette was named after. (He brought tobacco to England they say.) Sir Walter was a guest of the Tower for more than 12 years, the poor soul!

The comments above, plus writer has included more research; more details, more color; brings a personal perspective; adds his own brand of humor and imagination; but the piece could use a concluding line to tie up the ends.

Level 3 Example

There were many illustrious "guests" of the Tower of London. Let me tell you about some.

In 1297, William Wallace, a patriotic Scot, rebelled against the English rule in Scotland. He defeated the English at Stirling Bridge, but he himself was defeated at Falkirk in 1298. For the next seven years, he conducted a guerrilla campaign until 1305, when he was betrayed to the English and brought to London. Wallace was played by Mel Gibson in "Braveheart."

The deaths of Edward IV's two sons, Edward V and Richard Duke of York, also known as the Princes, is perhaps the saddest tale from the Tower's long and bloody history. The children were smothered in their beds, and the bodies were buried in secret. After this, the Garden Tower was renamed The Bloody Tower.

Sir Thomas More was a famous statesman and scholar, who served Henry VIII until the break with Rome. A Lord Chancellor, Sir Thomas More refused to acknowledge Henry VIII as supreme head of the English Church. He would not sign an oath either. More also protested the divorce of Catherine of Aragon, who had given Henry only one living child, Princess Mary. He was canonized.

Anne Boleyn, Henry VIII's second wife, was taken to the Tower on a charge of adultery. Catherine Howard, Henry VIII's fifth wife and the woman he called his "very jewel of womanhood," was also found to be untrue. She went the way of her cousin, Anne Boleyn; in 1542.

Robert Devereux, Earl of Essex, was one of Elizabeth I's favorite courtiers, but he rebelled against her and was executed on Tower Green. He was beheaded in 1601. The Essex Ring, now in Westminster Abbey, is said to have been given to him by the Queen. The queen told him that if ever he were in trouble he was to send it back to her and she would save him. From the Tower he tried to return it, but either it did not reach her or she ignored it.

Guy Fawkes was a famous leading conspirator in the Gunpowder Plot to blow up Parliament. And, finally, Sir Walter Raleigh was an explorer known for his expeditions to the Americas, and for bringing tobacco and the potato from the New World to the British Isles. A favorite of Elizabeth I, he certainly lost favor! He spent 12 years in the Tower on a charge of plotting against King James I. He found comfort in writing and making liquor. Raleigh was eventually executed in 1618.

Many thousands of people were tortured or died in the Tower, but these were the most famous guests of all. Most of them couldn't even keep their heads!

The comments above, plus writer adds much detail and fact; uses complex sentences, humor, and interesting facts (Mel Gibson); provides a quotation from her research; advanced vocabulary and phrasing, such as "conducted a guerilla campaign" and "the Tower's long and bloody history."

▶ TOTAL IMMERSION AND UNIT STUDIES

As you probably know, homeschooling can greatly benefit the gifted child. According to author Joan Franklin Smutny in her book *Stand Up for Your Gifted Child*, "A key frustration of many gifted kids is that they rarely get to delve into a subject in-depth [in an institutional school]. Just when they get really interested, they have to stop and move to something else. At home, they can keep going."

Some bright learners do best with **independent study**—when they are given a project and then are left to work on it in the way they choose and in the time they need. Gifted learners can often work independently at an earlier age and concentrate for longer periods. Some prefer parents to act as guides or mentors, providing suggestions and giving feedback when needed.

At home, you can also tailor the curriculum; expanding the subject to include your middle schooler's specific passion. As home educator Deborah Haydock observes, "Gifted children often have powerful 'callings' which, I believe, should be honored, despite how unusual they may seem. Having choice and control in our lives is important for all of us, and it seems very important for gifted children to follow their deep passions and needs."

The typical school schedule is another obstacle to educating a gifted child. Because bright children can have intense powers of concentration, breaking the day into 30- to 50-minute-long segments is frustrating for them. Take the case of Siobhán, who connects with her reading so intently that she does not want to drop it and take up something else at the ring of a bell. She doesn't want to break off her concentration or exploration or even "daydreaming" (read: creating).

Other characteristics of the gifted relating to study are:

- **They dislike drill and repetition.** They may know instinctively what researchers have found: Repetitive work shuts down higher brain functions.
- **Once they have grasped a concept, they have grasped it.** Sometimes a reminder is necessary to trip the memory, but repeated drill isn't.
- **It is rare to find a learner who is gifted across the board.** Your child may be gifted in one or several areas, but age-appropriate or delayed in others. Adapt your child's studies to fit this truth.
- **Gifted learners may learn some things very easily with little help from others.** They often learn basic skills more quickly, better, and with less practice. "I'd rather do it myself" can be a refrain.
- **They often prefer challenging tasks to elementary work.** They may change simple directions to more complex ones to keep interested.
- **They are original thinkers,** seeking new, unusual, or unconventional associations and combinations among information.
- **Their interests are both wildly eclectic and intensely focused.** They exhibit an intrinsic motivation to learn, find out, or explore and are often very persistent.
- **They want to share what they know.** They are eager to give reasons for everything.
- **They may do best in total immersion of a subject** (astronomy) **or topic** (the Milky Way).

In short, gifted students have a passionate interest in one or more subjects and would gladly spend all available time learning more about these topics if they could. This kind of learner is lucky to be homeschooling, where special needs and preferences can be met without affecting the classroom dynamic in a traditional school setting.

What Is Total Immersion?

Many gifted learners do not grasp a subject in chapters, but rather in volumes! These learners prefer **total immersion** in a topic or **in-depth studies**—perhaps including facts, theories, connections, associations, and an overall view. Gifted thinkers often process information differently. They might:

- be highly inquisitive, willing to examine the unusual
- display a questioning attitude that seeks information for its own sake as much as for its usefulness
- be able to process huge amounts of information at one time
- have a large storehouse of data about a variety of subjects, which they can recall quickly
- see relationships among seemingly unrelated objects, ideas, or facts
- attack complicated material by separating it into components and analyzing it systematically
- be good guessers and can readily construct hypotheses and "what if" questions

Researchers Stanley, Keating & Fox discovered in their 1974 study of giftedness that math is best taught to "math smart" kids in long sessions, only once or twice a week. And immersion, of course, is known to be an excellent way to learn a foreign language.

Further, creative thinkers may learn not by logical, sequential steps, but by randomly making connections that may not be apparent to others. In other words, a bright learner *may know how* to go from step *a* to step *b*, but may be more comfortable doing step *j* before step *b*, or *z* directly after *b*.

You, as your child's guide, can address these issues of total immersion, uninterrupted study, and creative thinking by exploring unit studies.

▶ UNIT STUDIES

Unit studies are perfect for gifted learners who love to immerse themselves in a subject or who love to explore connections. Unit studies focus on a topic of interest and follow that topic on as many paths and activities as possible—a cross-disciplinary journey.

Unit studies easily incorporate listening, reading, writing, speaking, and research skills by virtue of the limitless avenues open to exploration: books, games, field trips, software, oral history, the Internet, and so forth. In addition, experience indicates that learners who follow unit studies are apparently more self-motivated and retain more of what they learn.

One great way to start a unit study is simply to pay attention to the interests your learner expresses. Hazel tagged along to her mom's yoga class one night and was amazed at how flexible the people were. She had lots of questions about yoga, so they designed a unit study together based on Hazel's interests and some of her parents' ideas.

During the unit study, Hazel:

- took a Kundalini yoga class at the community center with a friend for six weeks.
- practiced yoga on her own and kept a journal charting her progress.
- adapted some of the positions she had learned to make them easier for her younger brother to do.
- interviewed a homeopath and a medical doctor to get more information about the health benefits of yoga.
- studied a translation of Patanjali's Yoga Sutras at the public library to learn about the spiritual roots of yoga practice.
- talked informally with a family friend from India about how yoga is connected to Indian culture, and later related the conversation to her mom.
- read books on yoga and did a presentation for her parents, describing the differences between the Kundalini, Bhakti, Jnana, Raja, and Karma schools of yoga.
- learned the origins of the Sanskrit words used to name yoga positions.
- taught a half-hour yoga workshop to some of the other learners in her homeschool group.

Here's another example: Leroy visited the Egyptian wing at the Metropolitan Museum of Art and became enamored of mummies. He and his parents selected several ways to explore the topic of mummies, which naturally led to other related topics. Eventually, the mummy unit study took on a life of its own. Leroy's activities soon included:

◆ reading books on mummification.
◆ watching (and discussing) a PBS series on ancient Egypt.
◆ making flash cards with new vocabulary and meanings.
◆ building a model pyramid, complete with tunnels, chambers, and sarcophagi.
◆ listening to an audio biography of King Tut.
◆ writing essays on mummies and on Cleopatra's life.
◆ creating a translation key for hieroglyphics and English.
◆ teaching his brother some hieroglyphics, so they could write to each other in code.
◆ baking the kind of flat bread that was eaten in ancient Egypt.

Unit studies lend themselves to adaptation for all ages and all levels of intelligence within the homeschooling family; therefore, resources and enthusiasm can be shared. Sibling teaching also happens—which means understanding of information is reinforced and passed on. And children promote their own ideas for expanding a topic, which may include reading, writing, research, giving presentations, and taking field trips.

If you are new to homeschooling, the idea of creating a unit study all by yourself may be overwhelming. You may find unit studies in kits, either at a school supply store, a homeschooling curriculum fair, or on the Internet. For example, Shamika and her dad recently finished a unit study on gardens, adapted from a curriculum they purchased from another homeschooling family after a friend gave them some seeds. The gardening unit included sections on vocabulary, biology, art, literature, and history. Shamika explored further by researching the plants and trees that are native to the Northeast, and then visiting her city's botanic gardens with her homeschooling group to see how non-native plants fared during the long winters.

For additional unit study assistance, take a look at these websites, modifying their exercises to your learner's abilities, learning styles, and interests:

◆ Educational Units and Lesson Plans: www.coollessons.org
◆ A to Z Teacher Themes: www.atozteacherstuff.com/themes

Here are some exciting sites compiled by homeschooling parents:

◆ The Four Wheelers' Unit Study Directory: www.thefourwheelers.com/units
◆ The Milstids' Unit Study for Everyone: www.gulftel.com/~lvhmskl/unit.htm
◆ Free Unit Study Links: http://home.pacbell.net/ransom/unitstudies.htm

Stretch That Imagination

Whether immersing themselves or exploring a short-term interest, bright children are always in search of new and stimulating activities. As a parent, it's not always possible (or affordable) to have new, challenging projects at your immediate disposal. If you encourage your learner to be curious and creative, you can often use common household items and library books to stretch imaginations. There should be no hard, fast, and correct answers or procedures—the more divergent, the better! Sometimes new problems, rather than solutions, will arise. Keep an open mind and allow the activities to be open-ended. Allow total immersion if it happens!

Here are some creative springboards:

If your bright child is interested in **sports**, try these activities:

Level 1: Watch a sport you have never seen before, on TV or in person. Learn all you can about it. Cricket and curling are two possibilities.
Level 2: Invent a possible sport, writing or drawing its logical rules, equipment, and uniforms.
Level 3: Teach and play your sport.

If your gifted learner is interested in **different cultures**, try these activities:

Level 1: Listen to an ethnic radio station or TV station. Pick up an Arabic or Italian or Chinese newspaper and explore it with your child.
Level 2: Especially with musical/rhythmic learners, listen to the "music" of the spoken words of a foreign language. Borrow some tapes from the library and listen to the music of that country. What is new to you?
Level 3: Research and plan a family meal using only recipes from another country, doing the planning, shopping, and cooking with a parent. Invent a dish using products similar to the national recipes.

If your student is interested in **current events** or **politics**, try these activities:

Level 1: Scour the newspapers or news stations for local and global problems.
Level 2: Analyze the articles or reports for solutions. Discuss how these possible solutions could filter down to affect you and your family's lives.
Level 3: Brainstorm your own possible solutions and discuss the pros and cons with your family. Write a letter to your congressperson, sharing your opinion about the best solution.

If your learner is interested in **inventions** or **how things work,** try these activities:

Level 1: Share a book about inventions, such as *Totally Absurd Inventions* (Vancleave) *Girls Think of Everything: Stories of Ingenious Inventions by Women* (Thimmish and Sweet) or about how things work, such as *Why Do Clocks Run Clockwise?, When Do Fish Sleep?,* and *Do Penguins Have Knees?* (David Feldman).

Level 2: Analyze the cross sections of things, such as those in *Stephen Biesty's Incredible Cross Sections* or *Star Wars: Incredible Cross Sections*. Draw the cross section of your family vehicle or an appliance or an invention of your own.

Level 3: Interview family and friends in order to design the "perfect" broom or stove or car or whatever!

If your homeschooler is interested in **Greek and Roman** topics, try these activities:

Art: Design a travel poster of ancient Rome. Design a poster comparing Greek and Roman script. Research the use of horses in ancient art.

History: Note similarities and differences in Greek and Roman myths (and compare and contrast them with Norse myths). Compare the lives of soldiers in ancient times with today.

Language: Develop a Latin computer game or board game.

Architecture: Build models of Greek and Roman houses.

Science/History: Discover the connections between the names of the planets and ancient history.

If your middle schooler is interested in **biographies,** try these activities:

Level 1: Read two biographies of people who had similar achievements or who were in similar fields. Some examples are Charles Lindbergh and Neil Armstrong; Benjamin Franklin and Thomas Edison; Martin Luther King and Martin Luther; Clara Barton and Mother Teresa.

Level 2: List the achievements and obstacles of each person. What do you think of these? What would you do differently in their places?

Level 3: Write a paper that compares the lives, achievements, and obstacles of the two people you selected.

Organizing Information for the Spatial Learner

In general, spatial learners are image-oriented and have a talent for creating and responding to visual patterns. They often read charts, maps, and diagrams well, and like to solve puzzles and mazes, build and invent machines, and build with Legos®.

If your child's dominant learning style is spatial, he may respond well to information that is presented in a graph or chart. Give him a chance to make his own maps, lists, and charts. This will help him develop the habit of organizing information in ways that are most useful to him.

Another strategy is color-coding. For instance, in teaching and reviewing parts of speech, color verbs red, nouns blue, adjectives green, and prepositions purple. Write flash cards for review in different colors.

To help build language arts skills, while you are reading together, emphasize visual clues on the page—drawings, photos, sidebars, or other graphics. Encourage your learner to relate the graphics to what is happening in material you are reading. While reading a chapter book without illustration, encourage her to visualize elements of the story or even draw them.

Playing games such as Pictionary® encourages visual communication, and memory games like Concentration help create and strengthen visual memory.

Mastering Study Skills

Not all gifted learners are strong in study skills: managing time, following a plan, taking good notes, and so forth. To meet the challenge of absorbing and transmitting information and understanding, your middle schooler should eventually master these skills. Most of them require modeling and a lot of practicing.

- ◆ *Manage time* effectively by creating and following a schedule for completing work.
- ◆ *Take effective notes* by differentiating between main and supporting ideas, between key facts and specific examples and details.
- ◆ *Manage projects* by breaking them down into manageable tasks.
- ◆ *Solve problems* by identifying the problem, brainstorming solutions, evaluating possible solutions, and evaluating the success of the chosen solution.

Especially when *reading* for information, the more experimenting and practice, the better your gifted learner will coordinate reading and remembering skills into a method that works best for her. Here are some techniques for her to try with written materials.

- ◆ skimming
- ◆ scanning
- ◆ reading ahead
- ◆ rereading
- ◆ summarizing
- ◆ retelling or paraphrasing

Skimming and Scanning Tricks

Gifted students, who may not be inclined to read everything word for word (because their thoughts move too quickly), can learn to skim and scan. Explain that people read materials at different rates, depending on their purpose for reading. They can *skim* material for the main ideas; they can *scan* material for details.

Skimming. Mention that most people skim newspapers and magazines because they don't have time for in-depth reading. Give your learner a short news article. Explain that newspaper and magazine articles are usually written with the topic sentence first, and that if he reads the first sentence of each paragraph, he is likely to get a sense of the article. Tell him:

- ◆ You have 30 seconds to skim this article. Remember, you are trying to get a sense of the piece. Skim by reading the title and the first sentence of each paragraph.
- ◆ Turn over the article and write a sentence or two that summarizes the article.

Scanning. Explain that scanning is a way to find specific information or detail. Hand your learner a classified ad page or a timetable. This is more fun with several people playing:

- ◆ You are going to scan this ad page (or timetable). You are trying to find a specific bit of information.
- ◆ I will read an item (or a destination) and you try to find the cost (or arrival time).

If you practice this technique over several sessions, your student should find that she becomes faster at finding information. Similar exercises can be done in various subject areas to reinforce facts and details.

Listening and Reading Comprehension

Some gifted middle schoolers have complex thoughts that they may not be able to express clearly. As parents, you can help by coaxing discussion—of books and movies, for instance—to encourage understanding, appreciating similarities among people and their concerns, exploring ideas, comparing and contrasting themes, and drawing conclusions. Prompt your homeschooler with questions:

- ◆ What do you think this is about? (*main idea/theme*)
- ◆ Have we seen this theme/main idea elsewhere? (*main idea/theme*)
- ◆ What proof do you hear/read here that _____? (*details/facts*)
- ◆ What information does the author/screenwriter share with us about _____? (*details/facts*)
- ◆ What do you think the author/director means to say here, between the lines? (*inference*)
- ◆ What can we infer from _____? (*inference*)
- ◆ Can you guess what this word, _____, means? (*vocabulary*)
- ◆ What clues are there to its meaning? (*vocabulary*)

For more reading comprehension techniques and practice—including searching for fact and detail, finding the main idea and topic sentences, and deciphering vocabulary from context—check out these books:

◆ *I Read It, but I Don't Get It: Comprehension Strategies for Adolescent Readers* by Cris Tovani and Ellin Oliver Keene. (Portland, ME: Stenhouse, 2000).
◆ *Strategies That Work: Teaching Comprehension to Enhance Understanding* by Stephanie Harvey. (Portland, ME: Stenhouse, 2000).
◆ *"You Gotta Be the Book": Teaching Engaged and Reflective Reading With Adolescents* by Jeffrey D. Wilhelm. (New York: Teachers College, 1996).

▶ ACTIVITIES, ACTIVITIES, ACTIVITIES

We have chosen several fun activities that enhance the development of information and understanding skills. Of course, feel free to adapt these activities to your middle schooler's maturity and abilities.

Five-Senses Vocabulary

Multi-sensory memorizing is very powerful with this activity. Two people work together. One acts as the "wordmaster" and holds the definition of a new word in his hand. The "actor" must use all five senses to set the word into her memory. For example, with the word *relinquish*, she might visualize someone giving up (relinquishing) a rose; she can smell the rose, kinetically show the action of letting go of the rose, and say (and hear) the definition out loud. After a few words, the wordmaster acts out the words in a different order so that the other person can review them.

Let's Get a Job!

Obtain two copies of a sample job or college application online or at a local business. Ask your homeschooler to fill out the form, being careful to read all directions and note how large the spaces to fill in are. Have one or two other teens or adults read and gently evaluate how form was filled out, as if they were hiring the applicant. Discuss improvements and redo the form if necessary. Applicant may want to discuss what is bad or good about the form itself.

Natural Inspiration

Look for natural science classes in "your own backyard": your garden, a community park, a pond or stream, the woods, the beach, a desert, the mountains. Grab a pair of binoculars, a compass, a blank book and some drawing and writing pencils, a nature journal, and a portable guidebook exploring animals, insects, plants, birds, or minerals. You can observe and write, draw, memorize poetry while sitting under a shady tree, journal, or enjoy the writings of naturalists such as John Muir and Rachel Carson. **Level 2:** Take a class or course having to do with nature or the environmental sciences. **Level 3:** Teach a lesson about nature or organize a Roots and Shoots group (see Take the Challenge! Box).

"Roots creep underground everywhere and make a firm foundation. Shoots seem very weak, but to reach the light, they can break open brick walls. Imagine that the brick walls are all the problems we have inflicted on our planet. Hundreds of thousands of roots & shoots, hundreds of thousands of young people around the world, can break through these walls. We CAN change the world."

—Dr. Jane Goodall, scientist

Roots & Shoots is an international environmental and humanitarian program for young people, driven by young people, begun in 1991 by 16 kids gathered on Jane Goodall's front porch in Tanzania, East Africa! Roots & Shoots members, from pre-kindergarten to university age, demonstrate their concern for living things through service projects in their communities and global connections, such as:

- "adopting" a beach or river
- building bird houses
- learning about and growing native plants
- starting recycling programs
- raising funds to sponsor an endangered animal

Explore these sites and others about Dr. Jane Goodall and her international Roots & Shoots groups. Why not start with their home page:

www.janegoodall.org/rs/index.html

The Roots & Shoots Network, semi-annual newsletter

http://vax.wcsu.edu/cyberchimp/roots/board.html

The Roots & Shoots Teachers' Corner

http://vax.wcsu.edu/cyberchimp/roots/teacher.html

Questions to Pursue:

- What work is Jane Goodall known for?
- How did Roots & Shoots begin?
- What is their mission and what are their three themes?
- What are some current projects?
- How do I start a Roots & Shoots group?
- What ideas can I come up with for projects?

"Step Lively on the Main Concourse"

Design and write a brochure of your neighborhood or mall and conduct a guided tour for family or visitors.

The Rain in Spain

You and your middle schooler (especially a rhythmic/musical learner) can make up games, silly songs, rhymes, or chants to remember geography. For example, "Maine's northeast of New Hampshire, New Hampshire's east of Vermont. Massachusetts is south of all three, and has great seafood restaurants!" Or you might read *Wish You Were Here: Emily's Guide to the Fifty States*—part travel diary, part atlas, this account of a girl's trip across the United States features maps and trivia about each of the 50 states. Software such as *Where in the World Is Carmen Sandiego?* and *The Complete National Geographic* add excitement to the process.

Carschooling®

There are a multitude of exciting learning ideas that can be implemented while traveling in the family car. Homeschooling mom and author Diane Flynn Keith calls this Carschooling® and she has a website all about it: www.homeschool.com/advisors/keith/default.asp. Here are a couple of car schooling activities, which the parent may modify as desired.

LICENSE PLATE SCRABBLE

The creatively gifted love this game; it also advances spelling, vocabulary, and word-order skills. The idea is to take three letters of a license plate and make them into a word, using the first letter as the first letter of the word, the second letter as any letter in the middle of the word and the last letter as, well, the last letter. For example, DSY can become "daisy" or "Disney" or "discovery."

Scoring: Each person getting a correctly spelled word earns a point. Or, the person making the longest word scores 3 points and the others score 1 point. In tournament play, the person forming the longest word gets the sum of the numbers on the license plate. You keep these totals on paper, and the first to reach 100 points wins.

License Plate Scrabble Variations:

◆ Allow the letters to be scrambled first and then make them into a word. Thus, if you see GHL, you could scramble it to LHG and come up with "laughing."

◆ Acronyms: Invent a real-sounding government agency or company with the three letters. For instance, OPA transforms into "Office of Pets Administration" or "Office of Peculiar Acronyms." If you get either a chuckle or groan from other participants, you score!

Webmaster

Design your own family website (learning from software or from the family propeller-head). Post your own and your friends' poetry, art, jokes, short stories, games, photographs, or other information. Add links to sites you admire and explain why you like them. Try doing the same with websites that you find ugly or hard to navigate, collecting your own list of "Awfully Bad Websites."

Let's Become Billionaires!

Use Monopoly® money or paper commodities and divide up into teams with your family or gifted students club. Take weekly buy and sell orders, record them, figure commissions, and do company research in the newspapers and on the Internet. Share what you understand from what you've read and heard and ask questions.

Alibi

This is a group game teaching questioning and observation skills. The group is told that last night the local bank (name it) was robbed around 7:30 P.M. Tell the group that two of them are going to be interrogated as suspects. Select two suspects, who will go to another room to create an alibi together—a concrete story of their whereabouts the night before. Then *one* suspect at a time comes back in front of the group and answers questions about the alibi. The "detectives" may take notes or draw sketches. The second suspect is brought in and questioned. If their stories match and the detectives find no slip-ups, then the suspects are free to go!

Academic Clubs

These clubs unify around a specific academic skill or subject, such as math, history, or environmental science. Some homeschoolers form their own clubs or, in some supportive school districts, home-schoolers join regular schoolers' clubs. One middle school, for example, offers a Weather Club. Students create daily weather maps using data from their own weather station and then broadcast their forecast on the local radio station. Competitive debate clubs help teens develop their public speaking, critical thinking, and language facility, and may lead to competitions around the country. Your child may create a homework club for co-op studying.

Summary

We live in what is called "the Information Age," although sometimes it seems like the information *overload* age! Data, facts, details, theories, opinions, and conclusions—all types of information bombard us. Ideally, we process, compare, evaluate, and understand the information we each need for our lives to run smoothly.

We strive for our children to learn to receive and transmit facts and ideas from all the amazing sources our exciting information age has to offer, including books, cassettes, billboards, newspapers, letters, radio, TV, Internet, and software.

▶ **PRACTICE** *(Keys, examples, and rubrics may be found in Appendix A)*

I. Biography

Compare two people with the same profession but who lived in different periods of time. Read something about the time periods of both. Explain how the time during which they lived affected their lives and efforts.

Examples:

Babe Ruth and Mickey Mantle
Abraham Lincoln and Lyndon Johnson
Gordie Howe and Wayne Gretsky

II. Gender Stereotyping

1. Find a magazine or textbook from at least 30 years ago (in the attic or garage or at the library). Tally the occupations of the two genders in the ads or illustrations. Describe how men and women seem to be viewed in the year of your research. OR

2. Do a comparative analysis of advertising directed to men (such as *Sports Illustrated* magazine) and women (such as *Ms.* magazine). How do these appeals differ?

III. Instructional Essay

Write an essay that describes in an engaging and novel way how to perform a complex task. Use your imagination—for example, being the shoelace that is getting tied!

4

Reading, Writing, Listening, and Speaking for Critical Analysis and Evaluation

GOAL: *Learners read, write, listen, and speak for critical analysis.* As listeners and readers, gifted students analyze experiences, ideas, information, and issues presented by others. As speakers and writers, they use oral and written language to give opinions on experiences, ideas, information, and issues.

METHOD: *Many gifted students use higher level thinking than their age peers.* Learners may excel in such activities as brainstorming, problem solving, association, and analysis.

M iko and her older sisters loved theater so much they often saw a play each month. During the ride home, the young women always critiqued the show they had just seen.

During one ride home, Miko suggested the family have a scale to compare plays. "Like the Olympic judging," she explained.

Her sisters quickly gave Miko the task of creating a scale. Miko began snatching the entertainment section from her mother's newspaper and reading the theater reviews.

During the next month, Miko's family thought she had lost interest in her idea. A week later, however, Miko handed out a description of a scale that ranked shows from 1 to 10. She also included examples of each rating. She explained that musicals should only be compared to musicals and comedies to comedies. Otherwise, she explained, it would be like scoring a gymnast and swimmer in the same event.

Gradually, Miko became the family's in-house critic. She would summarize reviews she had read whenever the family was deciding what show to see next. Her sisters were impressed with how objectively Miko would present the reviews. In honor of her, they named the scale "Miko's Scale of 1 to 10."

▶ Language Arts for Critical Analysis— What Do We Mean?

Is your gifted child like Miko—a keen and alert observer who is good at analyzing? All of us, in fact, are continually evaluating our experiences, at least to some degree, as we read a magazine, watch a commercial, select a DVD to rent, or listen to our mayoral candidate's campaign speech. We listen, we read, and we analyze to make judgments and decisions.

Gifted children may easily master **critical analysis** and evaluation, displaying the skills necessary to sort information, to use logic, and to construct informed choices. In fact, like Miko, your learner may be very comfortable with higher-level thinking skills, such as evaluating, making associations, brainstorming, and problem solving.

The down side is that a gifted child may be *too* analytical or *too* critical. Take Anne-Louise, who sometimes sounds rude and egotistical when evaluating others. Or Oliver, who is a perfectionist when evaluating himself. As a loving parent, you can guide the over-analyzer on a gentler route.

The up side is that you can help your gifted middle schooler refine such analytical qualities as:

- seeing patterns, relationships, and connections that others don't
- perceiving subtle cause-and-effect relationships
- needing a minimum of experiences for complete understanding
- processing abstract and analytical ideas

General Activities for Critical Analysis

Activities appropriate to this goal for your gifted learner include:

- ***Reading*** literature, advertisements, editorials, book and movie reviews, literary criticism, and political speeches
- ***Writing*** persuasive essays, book and movie reviews, literary critiques, editorials, thesis/support papers, analyses of issues, and practice college application essays
- ***Listening*** to advertising/commercials, political speeches, and debates
- ***Speaking*** to present book and movie reviews, persuasive speeches, opinion surveys, and conduct debates and interviews

What Skills Are We Looking For?

We are guiding our gifted middle schoolers to eventually master and excel in these language arts skills:

- Listening, reading, writing, and speaking to evaluate experiences, ideas, information, and issues within oral and written experiences (*Max critiqued his sister's monologue, using specific examples.*)
- Using evaluative criteria from different points of view (*Although Sally didn't enjoy the play, she said she could understand why Brian might.*)

- Recognizing the differences in evaluations *(For the audience at which it's aimed, Jennifer thinks the movie is well done.)*
- Recognizing bias, propaganda, or false claims—in ourselves and others *(After reading campaign literature from all three candidates, Liz changed her opinion about the mayoral election.)*
- Using the best oratory techniques in speech and debate *(Deirdre always begins her speeches with a question to get her audience's attention.)*
- Making decisions about the quality of texts and events, providing evidence and detail *(Ezra rejected the subtle persuasion of the sneaker commercial, which used celebrities and peer pressure to sell the product.)*
- Presenting arguments with appropriate support *(Sara and Emily continue to debate the pros and cons of buying the Suck-It-Up vacuum, based on ease-of-use, durability, and cost.)*
- Applying the rules of grammar, usage, spelling, and punctuation in persuasive writing *(Rachel corrected the use of semicolons in her essay on* Of Mice And Men.*)*

▶ EVIDENCE OF SUCCESS IN CRITICAL ANALYSIS

For a discussion of the five elements of growth in learning—range, flexibility, connections, conventions, and independence—please refer to page 43.

With your guidance, your middle schooler will move into mastery of language arts skills at her own rate, in her own best manner. So, how will you recognize mastery in critical analysis? Consider these accomplishments.

EXAMPLES OF MASTERY include
- identifying fact-versus-opinion in a magazine article
- writing a letter to a fast food chain or snack company, explaining why they should change the misleading photograph on a product's packaging
- using the standards of scientific investigation to evaluate a science lab experiment
- reading two conflicting reviews of a play, recognizing the different points of view
- in a poetry group, selecting the most important word of a poem and explaining its significance
- presenting an oral review of a film—referring to character development, plot, pacing, cinematography, and lighting
- writing about the effects of a hurricane from the perspectives of a working parent, an emergency worker, and a truck driver
- debating a social issue while following the rules for formal debate

EXAMPLES OF ADVANCED MASTERY include further development of the skills used previously and

- ◆ delivering a campaign speech, using a variety of persuasive strategies
- ◆ reading the writing of two or more critics on the same author and determining what literary criteria each used
- ◆ in a supportive group, critiquing each other's writing; revising text based on the group's suggestions
- ◆ reading a current article on a scientific issue, such as the greenhouse effect, and comparing it to an earlier article on the same issue
- ◆ writing two analyses of a Supreme Court decision—from the perspectives of a strict constructionist and a judicial activist
- ◆ listening to speeches of two political candidates and comparing their positions
- ◆ comparing critiques from two different centuries' productions of Shakespearean plays

Now let's examine a writing assignment and three sample responses. Throughout *Homeschooling Your Gifted Child: Language Arts for the Middle School Years*, you will find examples of two to three levels of mastery.

▶ Sample Exercise

Think about the convictions you hold concerning a community or political issue, such as pollution, deforestation, discrimination, drug use, or the draft. Finish the following sentence and then explain why in one or two paragraphs.

I am ready to stand up in a group and defend my beliefs in _____.

Examples and Comments

The following are two examples of successful answers to the given prompt, along with comments on each short essay.

Level 1 Example

I am ready to stand up in a group and defend my beliefs in requiring, by law, that big companies pay for cleaning up their own pollution and waste. The United States has a long history of manufacturers polluting the environment. For example, ammunition manufacturers in New York and New Jersey have polluted the underground water with arsenic, which was used in the making of gunpowder, I think. I heard on a TV documentary that it may take decades to clean this dangerous mess up. Also, the taxpayers usually have to pick up the tab without having started the pollution. Although, in a way, consumers started the pollution by demanding products that cause pollution in their manufacturing.

> *Writer understands the analytic stance asked for in the prompt; writer uses example and detail; word choice might be better ("corporation" for "big companies"); uses slang in an effective way, to match tone, such as "pick up the tab;" writer should use more than simple sentences; writer demonstrates logic.*

Level 3 Example

I am ready to stand up in a group and defend my beliefs in the inherent right of an American family to choose the best schooling for their children. Children are individuals who need individualized care and support, and only their families know them best. My cousin Ev did very well in a traditional school setting and he loved it, while my cousin June, an eclectic homeschooler, liked to "stamp out her own trail," as my Aunt Carole says.

Also, different families have different needs: A ranch or farm family may prefer to unschool their children, as they will learn from the myriad of experiences and chores around them. For instance, I knew a family in a remote town whose sons raised and sold chickens. The two boys did all the financing, buying, feeding, construction of coops, healthcare, and bookkeeping involved in breeding and marketing chickens. Yessiree! They even negotiated a loan with the bank! Can you believe that? Those kids learned about working with people of all ages, accounting, construction, and chicken breeding—actually, about *real life*, all in one fell swoop.

I will stand up any day for that kind of diversity in education!

Previous comments, plus: creative and energetic; essay has a beginning, middle, and end; paragraphs are well organized; writer has an impressive vocabulary ("inherent," "eclectic"); uses reasoning to build a case; uses appositive and a quotation; writes in a mixture of sentence types; uses humor.

▶ HIGHER-LEVEL THINKING SKILLS

All gifted learners are capable of advanced thought processes, but most especially logical/mathematical learners. These learners often enjoy ordered activities such as number and pattern games and logic problems.

Because your gifted child reasons quickly and often without regard to process, you may need to help the child break down and analyze the steps involved in critical thinking and problem solving. ("How did we get to that answer, do you suppose?")

Typical characteristics of gifted learners with regard to higher-level thinking processes include:

- ◆ **They are better able to construct and handle abstractions.** They draw inferences and grasp concepts that other children need to have spelled out for them. They readily see cause-effect relationships.
- ◆ **They may not need to watch you in order to hear what you are saying.** They can operate on multiple brain channels simultaneously, processing more than one task at a time.
- ◆ **Gifted children take less for granted, seeking the "hows" and "whys."** They can ask a million questions!
- ◆ **They are willing to entertain complexity and seem to thrive on problem solving.** Bright kids are elaborate thinkers, sometimes producing new steps, ideas, responses, and other embellishments to a basic idea, situation, or problem.

- ◆ *Gifted students will support findings with evidence.* They like to gather data as though they were professionals in the field, assuming an attitude of inquiry, rather than merely pursuing information.
- ◆ *They can be less intellectually inhibited than their age peers in expressing opinions.* They are often skeptical, critical, and evaluative; they are quick to spot inconsistencies.
- ◆ *Bright learners may have several primary learning styles.* See pages 4–5 on Gardner's learning styles and multiple intelligences.
- ◆ *They should be encouraged to develop their own assessment tools.* These learners are capable of developing rubrics and other methods to assess or analyze their own projects.

▶ BRAINSTORMING

The goal of brainstorming is to use divergent thinking to generate ideas and solve problems (see page 9 of the Introduction on divergent thinking). Imagine your family is brainstorming to decide how to use a quarter acre of land. Psychologist Sidney Parnes has devised six vital ground rules for such an idea-generating session as your family might hold:

1. *Defer Judgment.* Keep your mind open to new ideas. This is the most important of the brainstorming ground rules. Do not limit your options by criticizing or praising an idea at the brainstorming stage.

2. *Look for Many Ideas.* Your goal is to generate lots of ideas and find many paths. "Quantity breeds quality" is the theme.

3. *Accept All Ideas, However Far-Fetched.* Never reject an idea because it seems wild or crazy. A silly idea may just work after all, or it may inspire a truly astounding one.

4. *Make Yourself Stretch.* Don't quit with "OK, guys, those are all the ideas I have." Instead, push yourself beyond your usual limits. Awesome ideas may come late in the process.

5. *Take Time to Let Ideas Simmer.* When you tell someone you want to "sleep on it," you are following this guideline. Putting a problem aside and later coming back to it may generate lots of new thoughts.

6. *Search for Idea Combinations or "Be a Hitchhiker."* Combine ideas (*combinations*) or build new ideas off of old ones (*hitchhiking*).

▶ PROBLEM-SOLVING

Gifted students are flexible thinkers, able to come up with many alternatives and approaches to problem solving. They may like creative problem-solving programs (see the *Take the Challenge!* box on the next page), which can benefit gifted kids in several ways:

1. Teammates draw on reasoning skills and resourcefulness.

2. Teammates work together to solve problems, honing skills in both leadership and teamwork.

3. All students, but especially perfectionists, may see that failures and setbacks are essential to accomplishment.

4. When a solution that works is reached, self-confidence is boosted.

5. Students are called upon to give time and effort to do their share within the team.

In *Helping Gifted Children Soar* (Gifted Psychology Press), educator Dr. Carol Strip claims, "The whole process of solving complex problems can be very liberating for gifted children, because to come up with creative solutions, they get to think 'outside the box.' This kind of wide-ranging thinking comes easily for most gifted students. They feel at home dealing with complicated issues."

TAKE THE CHALLENGE!

Problem-Solving Challenge: Organ Donation. During the past 20 years organ donation has transformed from being a futuristic possibility to a present-time reality for thousands of people each year. However, despite the advances in technology, lists of ailing patients needing transplants continue to grow. For some, the hope of receiving a donor organ is almost zero. *Will further advances in technology alleviate the problem or make it worse? What ethical issues surround organ donation in the 21st century?*

You have just read one topic from the 2001–2002 round of the national creative problem-solving program called the *Future Problem Solving Program (FPSP)*. Founded by creativity pioneer Dr. E. Paul Torrance, FPSP stimulates critical and creative thinking skills and encourages students to develop a vision for the future. Its mission is "to teach students how to think, not what to think." FPSP features competitive, as well as non-competitive, activities. Check out current and past challenges at www.fpsp.org.

Other stimulating brain tasks are offered by *Destination ImagiNation, Marathon Creative, Invent America*, and *Odyssey of the Mind*. Some states or universities have their own versions, and some offer non-competitive challenges too. It may just take one teen or one parent to get a group started.

More competitive homeschoolers may be familiar with state and national competitions that focus on academic achievement. Homeschoolers have placed first, second, or third in several of the following:

- The National Spelling Bee
- National Geographic Geography Bee
- Knowledgemasters
- Math Counts
- Science Olympiad

Browse around in cyberspace to enjoy creative problem solving sites. Here are some places to start:

Destination ImagiNation
  www.destinationimagination.org
Marathon Creative
  www.marathoncreative.com
Odyssey of the Mind
  www.odysseyofthemind.com

Logic Problems

"When you have eliminated the impossible, whatever remains, however improbable, must be the truth."—Sherlock Holmes in *The Sign of the Four.*

Like Sherlock Holmes, many bright people love logic problems. Players devise different ways to go at these problems—maybe checklists, charts, or diagrams, or maybe figured entirely in their heads. Here is one for you and your learner to enjoy!

The Problem

One week five bachelors (Andy, Bill, Carl, Dave, and Eric) agreed to go out together to eat five evening meals on Monday through Friday. It was understood that Eric would miss Friday's meal because of an out-of-town wedding. Each bachelor served as the host at a restaurant of his choice on a different night. Use the clues below to determine which bachelor hosted the group each night and what food he selected.

1. Carl hosted the group on Wednesday.
2. The fellows ate at a Thai restaurant on Friday, and did not eat tacos the previous evening.
3. Bill, who detests fish, volunteered to be the first host.
4. Dave selected a steak house for the night before one of the fellows hosted everyone at a raucous pizza parlor.

The first step is to carefully read the entire problem. This usually consists of an *introduction* followed by a series of numbered *clues.* The introduction frequently contains significant information that is *not* mentioned in the clues. For example, from the above introduction, one can conclude that Eric was NOT Friday's host. The end of the introduction usually clearly specifies the objective of the problem. For example, in the above problem, the solver is asked to match each night of the week, Monday through Friday, with one of the 5 men and with the food he selected.

You may (or may not) decide to use this *solve chart* to organize the given information and to deduce conclusions. Your goal is to isolate the solution by elimination of all other possibilities.

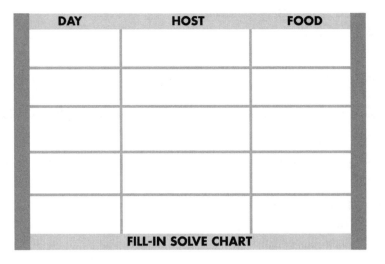

DAY	HOST	FOOD

FILL-IN SOLVE CHART

The Solution

There are other kinds of solve charts, but this fill-in chart is a good bet for this particular logic problem.

DAY	HOST	FOOD
Mon	Bill	Tacos
Tue	Dave	Steak
Wed	Carl	Pizza
Thu	Eric	Fish
Fri	Andy	Thai

1. Enter the 5 weekdays, Carl as Wednesday's host (Clue 1), Thai food on Friday (Clue 2), and Bill as Monday's host (Clue 3).

2. Pizza must be Thursday night or earlier. The only available row for Dave-Steak, which precedes pizza (Clue 4) is Tuesday. Thus Pizza is Wednesday.

3. Fish must be Thursday (Clue 3) and therefore Tacos are Monday.

4. Eric cannot be Friday (Intro) and so must be Thursday. Andy alone remains for Friday.

The bachelors problem was found at: www.geocities.com/Heartland/Plains/4484/logic. htm#where. There are many websites built just for logic problem lovers. Also, you will find an excellent list of tips for solving logic problems by William T. Pelletier at www.geocities. com/Heartland/Plains/4484/lptips.htm. Your gifted student can find more logic problems with an Internet search engine using the keywords "logic problems."

▶ ANALYSIS

Analysis includes many aspects of critical thinking, among them:

- ◆ forming an initial understanding
- ◆ making connections and associations
- ◆ understanding inference
- ◆ demonstrating a critical stance
- ◆ extending and applying what you know to something new

Forming an Initial Understanding

Forming an *initial understanding* precedes evaluation of, and response to, whatever we read or hear. Initial understanding means your learner has a first impression or *holistic* ("big picture") understanding of what has been read or heard. It involves considering the text as a whole or in a broad perspective. Questions to ask your learner regarding initial understanding might include:

1. After reading/hearing this, what do you think is the most important information?

2. What do you think is the best theme of this story/article?

3. What is this piece supposed to help us do or learn?

Making Connections and Associations

When Sylvia was five years old, she was asked what steam and ice have in common and she responded faster than the psychologist had ever heard, "water." That's associative thinking. You may have also noticed that your gifted thinker perceives similarities, differences, associations, and anomalies more than her age peers.

Gifted children tend to be fluent thinkers, able to generate possibilities, consequences, or related ideas. They may be able to make connections and associations between apparently unconnected ideas and activities. Among the many possible careers and hobbies out there, these children make good poets.

Imagery: Simile and Metaphor

Simile and metaphor are examples of imagery that connect two otherwise unrelated things: smoke and birds, or a beard and a cloud. Help your student learn poetic style by sharing examples of simile and metaphor in poetry and prose. Poets and children love these figures of speech and will often be able to readily imitate them.

> The blue smoke leaps
> Like swirling clouds of birds vanishing.
> —Richard Aldington

> His form like a king, his beard like a cloud.
> —Joaquin Miller

> I said, but just to be a bee
> Upon a raft of air
> —Emily Dickinson

> Then my elephant feet tripped over themselves.
> —anonymous 6th grader

Understanding Inference

Drawing inferences is an advanced thought process, which involves asking questions such as "What does this passage suggest?" "What do you think the author meant by . . . ?" Understanding inference (and inference questions on a test) challenges your learner because she will need to recognize implied—rather than directly stated—meanings in order to reach a conclusion. Encourage your student to be a detective, looking for such clues as:

◆ word choice
◆ tone

These clues suggest a certain conclusion, attitude, or point of view.

Your gifted learner should ask herself this question: "What evidence do I have that this is what is really meant?" In other words, the inference your middle schooler makes should be logical and based on details or something clearly implied—not on her bias or hunch.

For example, if your child reads a passage and then states, "Harry seemed sad after his meeting with Dumbledore," can she show *evidence* that Harry was sad? Did the writer use words like *weepy* and *despondent* or describe Harry sitting with his head in his hands?

Demonstrating a Critical Stance

Some gifted kids are very sensitive and have difficulty distancing themselves from something. However, demonstrating a critical stance requires readers and listeners to stand apart from a subject and consider it objectively. What tasks are involved in this?

◆ comparing and contrasting
◆ recognizing the organization of ideas
◆ discovering bias
◆ understanding irony and humor
◆ making connections between texts

What questions might you ask your learner to promote a critical stance? The following are a few ideas for analyzing a text or a speech:

1. Do you think the author/speaker has a bias?
2. Does the author/speaker use humor? images? special language? Explain.
3. How useful would this text/speech be for _____? Why?
4. What information could be added to improve the author's/speaker's argument? Explain.
5. Can you compare this text/speech to _____?

Extending and Applying What You Know to Something New

Some smart children are very adept at transferring concepts and learning to new situations. They may even make intuitive leaps toward understanding something new without necessarily being able to explain how they arrived there. These, once again, are high-level thinking skills that your middle schooler may possess.

The following is a set of exercises that demonstrates extending what you know to something new. As always, you the parent can add or take away elements to adapt the exercises to your child.

Proverbs

Begin by asking your middle schooler what a proverb is and ask for examples—such as "Slow and steady wins the race." Discuss an interpretation. Note that most cultures have their own proverbs. A search on www.amazon.com brings up books of proverbs from many cultures, including African, French, Czech, Chinese, Jewish, Scottish, and Swedish. One intriguing title is *A Fool in a Hurry Drinks Tea with a Fork: 1047 Amusing, Witty and Insightful Proverbs from 21 Lands and Languages.*

The Korean word for proverb is *Sok-dam* or "folk saying." Korean proverbs, just like English proverbs, provide us with humor and metaphor. And they are indirect lessons about ideals, such as integrity and cooperation. Here are some great analytical exercises involving proverbs.

Level 1: Analyze English Proverbs

Make a list of all the proverbs you can think of. (This is much more fun in a group.) Analyze what the proverbs mean. Rewrite the proverbs in terms more relevant to your own experience.

Sample proverbs:

- Don't cut off your nose to spite your face.
- He can't see the forest for the trees.
- Don't cry over spilled milk.
- Out of the frying pan, into the fire.
- Don't count your chickens before they're hatched.
- Haste makes waste.

Level 2: Analyze Korean Proverbs and Find Counterparts

You and your student or group read or recite the following Korean proverbs and try to decide what they mean. Write down or suggest English counterparts.

Example:
Korean: *Though it is small, the pepper is hot and good.*
English counterpart: *Good things come in small packages.*

1. Korean: *Speak of the tiger and it appears.*
English counterpart: _____

2. Korean: *Too many carpenters knock over the house.*
English counterpart: _____

3. Korean: *Seven falls, eight rises.*
English counterpart: _____

4. Korean: *Someone else's rice cake looks bigger.*

English counterpart: _____

5. Korean: *Starting is half done.*

English counterpart: _____

Answers

Possible English counterparts: 1. *Speak of the devil!*; 2. *Too many cooks spoil the broth.*; 3. *If at first you don't succeed, try, try, again.*; 4. *The grass is always greener on the other side.*; 5. *A stitch in time saves nine.*

Level 3: Read and Analyze *Aesop's Fables*

Many of our common proverbs come from *Aesop's Fables*. Read or peruse the fables and select morals that have interest. Then research to find—either online or in proverb books—proverbs with similar messages, but from other cultures. If you are a visual learner, you can enrich this activity by illustrating proverbs as you find them, creating a booklet of favorite proverbs.

▶ SOME THOUGHTS ON PERFECTIONISM

While your bright child is being analytical, is he being too critical of *himself*? Some gifted kids are **perfectionists**. Traits may include:

- ◆ worrying excessively over details
- ◆ judging himself harshly
- ◆ avoiding learning situations or new things for fear of failure
- ◆ finding it hard to accept criticism or to laugh at herself
- ◆ focusing on mistakes, rather than successes
- ◆ setting unrealistic goals, then berating himself for not reaching them
- ◆ procrastinating
- ◆ leaving work unfinished
- ◆ having difficulty starting a project, afraid his effort won't be good enough

If you feel you have a perfectionist child, you will need a lot of patience to convince her that you love and accept her for *who* she is, not *what* she achieves. You may even have to look at your own expectations or consider if you're a perfectionist, too!

Further, you will want to research and explore techniques to help your child enjoy *the process* and care less about *the product*, to celebrate creativity, to set realistic goals, to take risks, to know that mistakes are OK. Also, many homeschooling families do not assign grades, but rather evaluate progress—which is helpful to a perfectionist learner.

CRITICS' PICKS

Here are some favorite books from Clare Doyle, age 12, another middle schooler.

- *Because of Winn-Dixie* by Kate DiCamillo
- *The Giver* by Lois Lowry
- *Jacob Have I Loved* by Katherine Paterson
- *Marie Antoinette: Princess of Versailles Austria-France, 1769* by Kathryn Lasky
- *Nancy Drew* series by Carolyn Keene—the older ones (the first 50 or so) are especially good
- *Number the Stars* by Lois Lowry
- *A Series of Unfortunate Events* series by Lemony Snicket
- *The Tiger Rising* by Kate DiCamillo

Practice Critical Analysis

◆ Continually evaluate what you read, write, and hear, looking for clarity and good logic, supporting detail, comprehensiveness, and originality.

◆ Discuss differences in perspective in the world around us. For example, in considering whether to allow a factory into your community, one group might be enthusiastic about the additional jobs to be created, while others are concerned about the air and noise pollution that could result.

◆ Read a sports editorial and evaluate it together, considering accuracy, objectivity, comprehensiveness, and understanding of the game.

◆ Point out examples of propaganda techniques (such as "bandwagon," "plain folks" language, and "sweeping generalities") in public documents and speeches.

◆ Compare two different literary forms expressing the same theme, such as music lyrics and a story about the loss of a love.

▶ ACTIVITIES, ACTIVITIES, ACTIVITIES

These activities promote the development of analytical skills in gifted children—in all children! As usual, feel free to modify these activities to your middle schooler's maturity and abilities. You will find additional enrichment activities in *Basic Skills for Homeschooling: Language Arts and Math for the Middle School Years* (LearningExpress).

"Hitchpock"

This wonderful group game practices grammar, structure, and vocabulary, without the players' even realizing it! One player silently picks a verb in his head such as *scrub, listen, exaggerate,* and so forth. The word "hitchpock" substitutes for that verb, with the other players trying to guess the verb by asking questions such as

- Do you "hitchpock" every day?
- Is it easy to "hitchpock"?
- Can anyone "hitchpock"?
- Can you "hitchpock" the kitchen sink?

The holder of the verb can only answer *yes* or *no* to these questions. The person who correctly guesses the verb selects the next hitchpock.

Write a Television Plot

Discuss a favorite TV show—What does it offer you? Who are the most compelling characters? Why? Discuss the plausibility of current plots and relate them to your own personal experiences. Then write up a plot and two subplots for the same show.

Newspapers

Both print and online newspapers are great resources. Many online papers have learning activities and current event games or enrichment exercises for students. Three tricks to encouraging critical analysis:

- Read letters to the editor together and debate their merits and points of view.
- Compare coverage of a current news item in two or more papers.
- Read and discuss essays on the editorial pages.

Journalistic Style

Study an abridged version of the Associated Press Style Book or another journalistic style manual. Together, choose a few grammar or usage rules that a newspaper staff might vote on to unify their writing, such as the use of titles with names in a news story or when to use introductory commas. Award 5 points for each example of each of the rules found in two or more different newspapers, providing a reward at 100 points. If there are variances in style, which style do you prefer?

The World of Marketing

1. Write a letter to a manufacturer praising or complaining about a product. Use detail, example, and a positive tone. Make suggestions for improvement.

2. Rhythmic/musical learners may want to invent a catchy commercial jingle that the manufacturer could use to advertise their products or one of your own invention.

3. Design a humorous ad campaign to promote a product of your choice or one you have invented.

4. Enter a manufacturer's contest.

Speed Reader

If you are fascinated by the idea of reading faster, yet retaining more, take an online course or try a speed reading software, such as AceReader, where you can test your own speed and acquire speed reading techniques. Independent learners love to beat their own times!

Persuade Me

Watch a video or listen to audiotapes of famous speakers such as Martin Luther King, Cesar Chavez, or Eleanor Roosevelt. Identify and discuss the qualities that lead them to be great persuaders. Can *you* persuade your family or homeschooling group to do something? Try it in a five-minute speech, using appropriate tone, attitude, body language, supporting detail and reasons, and persuasive vocabulary. Before you start writing, ask yourself:

1. Who is my audience?
2. What message do I want to communicate?
3. What is my point of view (my bias)?
4. What evidence supports my opinion?
5. What is the best way to convince this particular audience?
6. What kind of response or action am I seeking?
7. How will I evaluate my own writing or speaking?

Analyzing Short Stories

- Review with your learner the elements of fiction: plot, setting, characters, theme, mood, and tone.
- Read a short story of appropriate complexity for your middle schooler. Read the story once for the general plot; read it again to identify the other elements of fiction.
- What are your opinions on the effectiveness of the different elements? Base your opinions on evidence from the story.
- After you have discussed two or more short stories, compare their strengths and weaknesses to each other.
- Graphic/spatial learners might create and design awards for the stories: the Cliff-Hanger Award for the story with the most suspense, etc.

Summary

In a world flooded with media, we want our youth to be discriminating. We want them to be especially skilled in separating fact from rumor and in recognizing bias, propaganda, and point of view. In order to make wise decisions, they need to gather information and to analyze experiences and ideas.

Finally, our learners need to present their opinions and defend their judgments in satisfying and appropriate ways; for example, to deliver a cogent argument, supported with detail (simultaneously a parent's trial and pride). Exposure to a variety of experiences and the modeling of making fair evaluations are two of the major paths we have explored in this chapter.

▶ **PRACTICE** *(Keys, examples, and rubrics may be found in Appendix A)*

I. Fantasy Future
Write about a dream job for yourself. It can be a fantasy job.

Level 1: Describe what your dream job is, where it is, what your duties and rewards would be. *(EXAMPLE: I would like to be the first female astronaut on a Mars base because . . .)*

Level 2: *Add to your essay:* Who would you like to talk with about this dream job and why? The person you choose can be dead or alive, real or fabled. *(EXAMPLE: I would talk with H.G. Wells because . . .)*

Level 3: *Add to your essay:* How could you make your fantasy future come true? *(EXAMPLE: I could start by earning money to attend Space Camp in Alabama by selling friendship bracelets and weeding gardens . . .)*

II. What's in a Name?
An old proverb says "A good name is rather to be chosen than great riches." Probably one of the greatest and most respected names of the twentieth century is Winston Churchill. After World War II was over, a worldwide banking company came to Churchill and offered him shares of stock worth many millions of pounds, just for the privilege of using his name in the company's title.

Sir Winston quickly replied, "I do not wish your money. Such as it is, my name is not for sale."

Level 1: What do you think of this story? Do you agree or disagree with Churchill's decision? What would you do if the Coca-Cola Company or Nike offered you a million dollars for your name?

Level 2: Until about 700 years ago, in the days of King Richard the Lion Heart, most people went by a single name only, such as Arthur. They had no second name, later called a *family name* or *surname*. Sometimes the name of a place or an occupation was added for identification, such as Catherine of Kingston or Sam the Miller. Eventually, places or occupations became surnames: Kingston, Miller, Hill, Bush, Carpenter.

List the ten most common surnames in America. Where did you look or ask? What could be other sources for such a list?

Level 3: Many of us have first or last names that have been passed down for generations. What is your full name? Do you have three or four names? Interview relatives to find out how you got your name(s) and write down your findings. You may choose to tell your name story as a poem or short story or drawing of a family tree.

5

Reading, Writing, Listening, and Speaking for Literary Response and Expression

GOAL: *Learners read, write, listen, and speak for literary response and expression.* Gifted students read and listen to oral, written, and electronic texts and performances from American and world literature, relating these to their own lives; they develop an understanding of diverse social, historical, and cultural dimensions. As speakers and writers, learners use oral and written language for self-expression and artistic creation.

METHOD: *Many gifted learners excel in using creative processes.* Many gifted home-schoolers experience creativity through a more organic (inborn) than cognitive (learned) path.

*T**omas is confident* about his reading and writing abilities, less so about his conversational skills. His father, Hector, was pained to see that during youth group activities, Tomas could be found by himself, reading from a paperback book.

After the last group activity, an evening spent bowling, Hector asked Tomas what he liked and did not like about the evening. Tomas said he hated the time before everyone started bowling. "I want to talk with people, but I never know what to say," Tomas explained. "I guess I don't think fast enough."

"It seems to me you think pretty quickly," Hector said. "Speaking is a skill that grows stronger with practice, like bowling." But Tomas would not allow himself to be encouraged.

Hector saw a chance when he read that the youth group's annual gathering would be in Montreal, about six hours' driving time from his home. Tomas desperately wanted to attend.

"What are you going to contribute to the group?" his father asked. Hector saw that Tomas was stumped. "Maybe you could create something to help your friends remember the conference."

A short story fan, Tomas decided to write a short story based on the gathering. Hector liked that idea. "Maybe I could read it at the next meeting," Tomas offered hesitantly.

"That," his father said, "would be a wonderful gift to give your friends."

▶ WHAT DO WE MEAN BY LITERARY RESPONSE AND EXPRESSION?

The story of Tomas illustrates some possible drawbacks of giftedness. Some gifted people are shy or maybe not as adept in one area of communicating as in another. Tomas is a creative thinker, but a shy speaker.

As a parent you may have already learned how best to motivate creativity in your child. One method is by connecting with someone else's creative works, works of literature such as novels, plays, poetry, folk tales, short stories, and songs.

Creatively gifted individuals respond to and express literature through a more *organic* (inborn) than *cognitive* (learned) path. They may create art or music or dance or literature "without a blueprint," incessantly and with passion. As writers and readers, they may intuitively understand the conventions of literature: allusion and metaphor, character arcs, plot, and wordplay. (Many bright people love puns, anagrams, crosswords, and palindromes.).

Appreciating literature, responding to it, and creating literature—**literary response and expression**—are truly among the great joys of life. Really, literature does no less than transmit human thought across cultures and centuries, reflecting the differences and similarities among societies and eras. It expresses the human imagination and the human condition. What a joy it can be to guide our learners into such lifelong pleasure.

General Activities for Literary Response and Expression

Activities appropriate to this goal for your gifted learner include:

- ◆ *Reading* stories, myths, fables, legends, poems, literary essays and criticism, plays, and novels
- ◆ *Writing* personal responses, interpretations, literary analyses, critiques, and original stories, sketches, poems, and plays
- ◆ *Listening* to oral readings of literature; attending plays and films
- ◆ *Speaking* for recitations of literary passages, dramatic presentations, and group discussions of literature

What Skills Are We Looking For?

We are guiding our gifted middle schoolers to eventually master and excel in these language arts skills:

- ◆ Identifying the features of major literary genres, using those features to interpret works *(Cody explained why Don's ideas would make a better short story than a novel.)*

- Reading and viewing texts and performances from a broad range of authors, subjects, genres, periods and traditions, and cultures *(Ava and her dad read Jane Austen's "Emma" together, then compared it to the modern movie "Clueless.")*
- Using inference and deduction to comprehend text *(Because of the foreshadowing throughout the book, Tyrone had already guessed how it would end by the time he reached the last chapter.)*
- Creating their own stories, poems, essays, plays, and songs using the elements of the literature they have read, with appropriate vocabulary *(Diana liked Pablo Neruda's poem so much that she used the first line as a jumping-off point to begin a poem of her own.)*
- Understanding and evaluating the literary elements of setting, character, plot, theme, and point of view and comparing those features to other works and to their own lives *(Etta thinks the complicated plot lines and characters of a Robert Altman movie are like her family's reunion.)*
- Recognizing different levels of meaning *(Brandy explains that the poet's images describe more than her literal physical beauty.)*
- Identifying significant literary devices: metaphor, symbolism, foreshadowing, dialect, rhyme, meter, irony, climax, and so forth *(Jay realized that there are many symbols in* Lord Jim *that show his inability to take action.)*
- Reading aloud with expression, conveying the meaning and mood of a work *(Jimmy recites the King's speech to Hamlet in a gruff voice.)*

▶ EVIDENCE OF SUCCESS IN LITERARY RESPONSE AND EXPRESSION

For a discussion of the five elements of growth in learning—range, flexibility, connections, conventions, and independence—please refer to page 43.

How will you recognize mastery in literary response and expression? Consider these accomplishments:

EXAMPLES OF MASTERY include

- identifying fact-versus-opinion in a magazine article
- reciting a favorite poem and telling why it's a favorite, conveying its meaning and effect
- choosing which books to read from a broad palette and keeping a reading inventory
- writing stories or poems for peers or siblings
- using references to literature to support a position
- retelling a familiar fairy tale or myth, in an individual style
- performing dramatic readings or recitations of stories, poems, or plays
- writing a sequel to a story, continuing the development of the characters, plot, and themes
- writing a review of a book to recommend it

◆ pretending to be a character in a historical story and writing letters about the character's life

◆ writing reviews of one work from different cultural points of view

EXAMPLES OF ADVANCED MASTERY include further development of the skills used previously and

◆ reading poems of different forms, including sonnets, lyrics, elegies, narrative poems, and odes, and recognizing the effect of the structure and form on the meaning

◆ acting out scenes from a full-length play

◆ writing interpretations, including a discussion of the principal features of the genre, the period, and the tradition.

◆ reading literary pieces on a common theme from several literary periods (such as Renaissance, Neo-Classical, Romantic, Realistic, Naturalistic, and Contemporary) and comparing the treatments of the theme

◆ reading and interpreting works from several world cultures and recognizing the distinguishing features of those cultural traditions

◆ viewing stage or film productions of a major play or novel and discussing the interpretation of the work

◆ writing stories or poems using stanzas and chapters, metaphors, foreshadowing, symbolism, and different forms of dialogue and narration

▶ SAMPLE EXERCISE

Instrumental music may describe an action, tell a story, or simply express the joy of musical sound. A composition can serve as a backdrop for a movie or cartoon, or it may exist for its own sake.

Your assignment is to listen, with your eyes closed, to a piece of instrumental music that tells a story, like "Peter and the Wolf" or "The Sorcerer's Apprentice." Be aware of themes that repeat, of contrasting sounds, and of various instruments. Write something that explains the piece or that expresses how you feel when you listen to it.

▶ EXAMPLES AND COMMENTS

The following are two examples of successful responses, along with comments on each. The first is an example of a creatively written report; the second is a poem inspired by the composition.

Example of a Creative Report

Peter and the Wolf was composed by the Russian Sergei Prokofiev (1891–1953). It is his sixty-seventh work, which we musical people refer to as "Opus 67." The famous tale of Peter and the Wolf is very popular among children around the world. The tale was translated into a musical piece by Prokofiev for his children.

Each character is represented by an instrument or instrumental family, and the entire piece combines all of the instruments into a magnificent symphony. Prokofiev's music imitates the movement and the qualities of Peter, his grandfather, the cat, the bird, the duck, the wolf, and the hunters.

The conductor reads the narration in between musical sections. Peter is the main character in this story. He is a little boy who lives in Russia, right on the edge of a meadow. Peter is very curious about the meadow, even though a dangerous wolf lives there, so he goes against his grandfather's will. Peter is represented by the string section. Peter's grandfather is represented by the bassoon. Will Peter get hurt? Will Peter ever listen?

The bird in the story is constantly flying away from and fighting with the cat and the duck. The bird is represented by the flute. The duck fights with the bird—they make fun of each other. The duck is represented by the oboe. The cat tries to eat the bird, but does he accomplish this task? The cat is represented by the clarinet. All their relationships are connected. The wolf tries to eat the cat, bird, duck, and Peter, but does he? The wolf is represented by the French horn. The hunters try to kill the wolf before the wolf kills Peter. The hunters are represented by the percussion. Do the hunters make it in time? Why don't you listen to "Peter and the Wolf" and find out!

Essay provides entertaining detail about the composition, its composer, and the tale; writer uses humor, repetition ("the _____ is represented by the _____"), advanced vocabulary and sentence structures; writer understands the connections among the characters and between the characters and the instruments; creative use of questioning, with a "surprise ending."

Example of Creative Expression

"Haiku of The Sorcerer's Apprentice"
Ever streaming gush,
Water overflowing, Stop!
Boots filled, water logged.

Writer understands Haiku form (Japanese form of poetry, 5-7-5 or 5-7-7-5 syllables, non-rhyming, using words of the senses); has grasped the narrator's situation and desperation in the poem; uses humor and expressive word choice.

▶ HOW DO WE TEACH AND PRACTICE THESE SKILLS?

Javonte is only 11, yet he is comfortable within the worlds of cyberspace and educational software, distance learning, educational cable TV, and books on tape. As parents, we find ourselves lucky to have so many resources to help us teach reading, writing, listening, and speaking for literary response and expression. There are a zillion websites, it seems, with lesson plans, games, quizzes, and entire books online! One example to explore is called "Jumpstart on Shakespeare for Junior High," at www.ncte.org/teach/Snow29431.shtml. This site, like many, applies to the traditional classroom and is easy to modify and enrich for your gifted homeschooler. There are so many ways for us to nurture creativity.

► NURTURING CREATIVITY

"Throughout the ages, cultures have been passed from one generation to another through the arts," claims creative giftedness educator Dr. Jane Piirto. "Music, drama, visual arts, creative writing, and dance can fill the need for creative expression, while aiding in stress management for high-achieving, high-energy-level children." The creative process seems to be more an emotional journey than a cognitive (learned) one.

If creativity is to be nurtured among our gifted children, the necessary risk-taking and openness to experience, demand a safe environment in which to explore. Trust is important here; that is, no child (or adult, for that matter) who is experimenting with creativity should be belittled or criticized, but rather encouraged with enthusiasm. All learners should be permitted to fail as well as to shine.

What Is the Creative Impulse?

Let's examine the creative process in adults, as analyzed by Dr. Piirto, who writes that the creative and productive adults she has studied have creative processes that fall into thirteen categories. (A few of the categories may already apply to a creatively gifted child.) Creative and productive adults

- seem to have rituals; for example, they like to walk.
- may crave silence.
- go to retreats and colonies.
- are inspired by travel.
- use imagination.
- trust their dreams.
- seek solitude so they may go into a state of reverie (or flow).
- fast.
- meditate.
- get inspiration from the muse.
- are inspired by others' works of art, science, and music.
- improvise.
- if they are "blocked," they read or write self-help books.

To jumpstart the creativity in all of us, Piirto recommends:

- Explore the joys of good conversation, maybe starting a monthly salon.
- Walk into a beautiful and silent church with symbolic stained glass windows to meditate on the spirit.
- Visit a cemetery to meditate on life.
- Hike in nearby nature parks to meditate on nature.
- Go to an art museum to meditate on beauty.
- Try to find your "domains of passion," that which you can't *not* do.
- Browse at a bookstore or a library.

◆ Attend a live concert, a play, a poetry reading, or a lecture to honor the creativity of others.

Of course, back at home, parents can nurture creativity in a panorama of ways.

How Parents Can Enhance Creativity in Children

◆ Provide a private place for creative work to be done.

◆ Allow daydreaming or reflection.

◆ Provide materials (e.g., musical instruments, sketch books).

◆ Encourage and display the child's creative work, but avoid overly evaluating it.

◆ Do your own creative work and let the child see you.

◆ Pay attention to what your family mythology is teaching.

◆ Value the creative work of others.

◆ Avoid emphasizing gender-role stereotypes.

◆ Provide private lessons and special classes when you can.

◆ Help children find outlets and audiences; pair them with creative adult mentors.

◆ Get creativity training.

◆ Find ways of turning destructive behavior into constructive behavior rather than relying on punitive methods of control.

◆ Encourage children to explore their universe from many perspectives.

◆ Emphasize that talent is only a small part of creative production and that discipline and practice are important.

◆ Encourage natural curiosity and the need to ask zillions of questions.

◆ Allow the child to be "odd," avoid emphasizing socialization at the expense of creative expression.

◆ Interact with the child with kind humor.

◆ Allow opportunities for children to make meaningful decisions.

◆ Provide open-ended learning experiences—those without a single right answer or method of exploration.

◆ Find creative ways of resolving conflicts.

◆ Let your child help give your family purpose, commitment, and courage.

▶ HOW TO STIFLE CREATIVITY

On the other hand, educator E.P. Torrance has written a sure recipe for killing a child's creativity (or what NOT to do):

- *Insist that children do things the "right way."* Teaching a child to think that there is only one right way kills the urge to try new ways.
- *Pressure children to be realistic, to stop imagining.* Labeling the child's flights of fantasy as "silly" will bring the child down to earth with a thud.
- *Make comparisons with other children.* This is a subtle pressure to conform, yet the essence of creativity is the freedom to conform or not to conform.
- *Discourage curiosity.* Brushing a child's questions aside translates to "your questions don't deserve respect."

► MATH-SMART GIFTEDNESS

Some gifted learners, especially those with "math-smart" giftedness, may begin reading later than other age peers. Typically, math-smart kids excel in math, advanced reasoning, applications, rhythms, music, and computers. (They may, of course, be advanced in other areas too, or not.)

In their early years, math-smart kids often reject reading and/or writing English because it doesn't fit into any orderly system they acknowledge. After all, English is a tough language to learn to spell and pronounce. For example, think of the six ways to pronounce "ough" in English: en*ough*, c*ough*, th*ough*t, b*ough*, thr*ough*, and alth*ough*) These "late" readers usually take off with a vengeance when they find subjects they want to investigate.

► WRITING POETRY

Many gifted kids love word play and singsong and rhyme. They may even create raps songs or poems to learn rote work. To augment this, parents can encourage such poetic forms as cinquains, haiku, couplets, and limericks. Here are some activities.

Cinquain Poetry

Kids usually love *cinquain poetry*, which has form but does not rhyme. This one was written for a Valentine card:

Valentines
Red, fun
Giving, getting, sharing
We are all happy.
Hearts!

To introduce cinquains, have your student copy down the following:

1 word, my topic: _____

2 adjectives: _____ _____

3 verbs: _____ _____ _____

4 describing words or a statement: _____ _____ _____ _____

1 describing word or a synonym: _____

To Rhyme or Not To Rhyme?

Help your learner accept poetry in both rhyming and non-rhyming forms. Compare poetry and the affect it has on your reader. For example, first read this rhyming poem by Marco Annunziata:

> **Fog**
>
> *The shrouded moon held hammocked*
> *in the clotted autumn night.*
> *The tangled fog unravelled,*
> *and whispered out the light.*

Then read another poem about fog, this one by Carl Sandburg:

> **Fog**
>
> *The fog comes*
> *on little cat feet.*
> *It sits looking*
> *Over harbor and city*
> *On silent haunches*
> *And then moves on.*

Discuss which you like best, if either, and why. Rhymes are pleasing and fun to write but may be challenging for some children. To initiate, here are some ideas:

- ◆ Have your learner think of rhyming words and rap songs.
- ◆ Read poems, songs, even nursery rhymes together.
- ◆ Recite rhyming verse out loud.
- ◆ Write limericks.
- ◆ Compose two-line couplets.

Here are some favorite books from Jordan Halpern, age 14, another middle schooler.

- *Animal Farm* and *1984* by George Orwell
- *Do Androids Dream of Electric Sheep?, The Game-Players of Titan, The Man in the High Castle, A Maze of Death,* and *Ubik* by Philip K. Dick
- *Foucault's Pendulum* and *The Name of the Rose* by Umberto Eco
- *Ghost World* by Daniel Clowes
- *His Dark Materials* trilogy by Philip Pullman
- *Interview With the Vampire* by Anne Rice
- *Maus* and *Maus II* by Art Speigelman
- *The Metamorphosis and Other Stories* by Franz Kafka
- *Neuromancer* by William Gibson

▶ LITERATURE-BASED READING

Literature-based reading promotes the use of original, complete texts, not condensed or excerpted versions. There are many exciting paths to follow when beginning with an original piece of literature.

As you read a novel or biography, for instance, one activity your bright homeschooler might like is to consider and describe predictions about what is going to happen in the story. These predictions can be written down and used later for discussion. Also while reading through the story, your student might identify and research vocabulary words that are new or unclear.

Once your story has been completed, your learner might select among these varied and creative activities while studying plot, character, and setting:

Plot
- *Mapping*: drawing a series of pictures of key elements of the story in the proper order
- *Collage*: photos, magazine clippings, headlines, or other items that demonstrate the story plot
- *Folded sequence*: a sheet of paper folded into thirds, one picture on each third of the paper demonstrating, in order, the introduction, climax and conclusion of the story
- *Timeline*: a linear chart in time increments (hours, days, weeks, etc.) indicating key actions in the plot
- *Cartoon strip*: a sequence of drawings similar to a newspaper cartoon

Character
- *Mobile*: a mobile of descriptive words or magazine pictures about the main character
- *Creative dramatics*: family or support group members gather in costume as a character, make a presentation about who the character is and what happens to the character, and answer questions about the story
- *Diary*: rewriting the story in the first person from the main character's point of view

Setting

- *Diorama*: a three-dimensional depiction of the setting in the story
- *Poster*: a large drawing of one of the scenes where the action takes place
- *Maps*: the geographical setting and the route characters take in a travel or adventure story

Some Recommendations for Literature-Based Reading

If you can go online, you have discovered by now that there are amazing resources available on the Internet. For instance, without even driving to the library, you can print out the full text of 20 of the greatest American short stories and even complete novels on Aaron Ezis's site at www. americanliterature.com/MAIN.HTML. Of course, visit the library too and practice research skills. See also LearningExpress' *Basic Skills for Homeschooling: Language Arts and Math for the Middle School Years* for reading resources, including a list of short story collections for middle schoolers by subject area.

One website recommends these classic stories for the gifted reader, grouped according to challenge level—but these groups are fluid.

Level 1

- *Alice in Wonderland* by Lewis Carroll
- *Anne of Green Gables* by L.M. Montgomery
- *Beatrix Potter's Tales* by Beatrix Potter
- *A Christmas Carol* by Charles Dickens
- *The Prince and the Pauper* by Mark Twain
- *The Princess and the Goblin* by George MacDonald
- *The Secret Garden* by Frances Hodgson Burnett
- *The Story of King Arthur and His Knights* by Howard Pyle
- *The Wind in the Willows* by Kenneth Grahame
- *The Wonderful Wizard of Oz* by L. Frank Baum

Level 2: *When your reader is ready, more advanced readings include*

- *The Hound of the Baskervilles* by Sir Arthur Conan Doyle
- *The Legend of Sleepy Hollow* by Washington Irving
- *The Monkey's Paw* by W.W. Jacobs
- *The Celebrated Jumping Frog of Calaveras County* by Mark Twain
- *The Outcasts of Poker Flat* by Bret Harte
- *The Ransom of Red Chief* by O. Henry
- *The Lottery* by Shirley Jackson
- *The Red Badge of Courage* by Stephen Crane
- *The Tell-Tale Heart* by Edgar Allan Poe

Level 3: *When your reader is ready, more advanced readings include*

- *Antigone* by Sophocles
- *Hamlet* by William Shakespeare
- *Huckleberry Finn* by Mark Twain
- *The Iliad* by Homer
- *Julius Caesar* by William Shakespeare
- *Uncle Tom's Cabin* by Harriet Beecher Stowe
- *Macbeth* by William Shakespeare
- *Romeo and Juliet* by William Shakespeare
- *A Tale of Two Cities* by Charles Dickens

TAKE THE CHALLENGE!

Literature-Based Reading. Take the challenge by reading works in their original English form —not excerpts or condensations:

- short story collections
- poetry collections
- classic novels and plays
- Newbery medal winners for young adult fiction
- Pulitzer-prize winning books and plays
- works that speak to your interests and passions

Explore these sites and others concerning literature-based reading:

Handbooks for the Young Reader's Choice Awards, youth division (about grades 4-8) and senior division (about grades 9-12).

www.ucalgary.ca/~dkbrown/yrca_samp.html

Sundance Publishing website. Here you will find literature-based learning materials to teach reading skills and language arts to students from pre-kindergarten through high school.

www.sundancepub.com

American literature classics. Entire works to print out and analyze. Some editor comments and essays too.

www.americanliterature.com/MAIN.HTML

Questions to Pursue While Reading Literature

- What is a classic in literature? Why do classics endure?
- In my opinion, what makes this particular work universal or not universal?
- What from the author's life is brought into his/her work?
- How would I use art to best capture the spirit of this work? (*Moby Dick* might be a turbulent oil painting; *Little Women* might be a quilt.)

Five Tips for Writing About Literature

You and your gifted child might consider adapting some of these helpful tips for writing or speaking about literature:

1. **Be straightforward and specific.** Introduce your topic in a straightforward, natural way, not as an answer to a given assignment. In the first few sentences, suggest why the subject is significant or interesting. Do not make claims that are too sweeping. *End the first paragraph with a strong and clear statement.*

2. **Be clear.** Each paragraph of the paper should develop some aspect of the theme. The aim should be to clarify and illustrate main points as the essay proceeds. Check for clarity by reading in succession the first sentence or two of each paragraph. Do they signal the logical development of the essay? If this quick reading does not show an argument-in-progress, rewrite the paper.

3. **Analyze, don't paraphrase.** Do not let plot summary or paraphrasing substitute for literary analysis. Concentrate instead on *significance* or how speeches and actions shape the understanding of events and characters. How are you moved emotionally? How do word choice, imagery, and rhythm communicate more powerfully than statement alone?
   Remember that in great literature:
   - ideas and issues are usually presented from complex perspectives.
   - conflicts within the writer or the writer's culture may be reflected in the text.
   - form is as important as content.

4. **Support your opinions.** Remember to provide evidence for your personal responses by quoting the text. Check that quotations really support your theme. Learn to work short quotations into sentences to enrich the reader's awareness of the significant phrases in the text.

5. **Give an interesting conclusion.** Do not make the conclusion a needless repetition of previous topic sentences. All too many essays end with a mechanical list of points already made. Instead, use the final paragraph to take your main point farther or to draw out the significance of the topic.

For more ideas on writing about literature, take a look at some Sample Book Ideas for Literature-Based Reading Enthusiasts (www.ucalgary.ca/~dkbrown/yrca_samp.html), featuring books that have been nominated for the Young Reader's Choice Award.

Listening Logs

Here's the activity: At stopping points during a read-aloud session, listeners react to the literature by writing in a journal or log. This exercise allows your learner to listen to literature, to personally respond, and to have a meaningful opportunity to write. Adjust the exercise as appropriate, but it is most interesting when you:

1. Tell your child that you will be stopping after reading a passage to ask her to write down some reactions. You will provide the prompt. She should listen for setting, basic plot, and main character development.

2. Read aloud a high-interest novel or short story for 15 or more minutes, maybe three times a week.

3. Stop at a logical spot (pre-arranged with your listener is OK), and ask a question concerning the passage you just read. You might select from these ideas:

Setting

- ◆ What does the setting remind you of?
- ◆ Write about a similar setting you have seen.
- ◆ What kinds of characters do you imagine would live there?
- ◆ How is the setting different from our town?
- ◆ Why do you think the story is set when and where it is?
- ◆ How would you make the setting more interesting?

Plot

- ◆ What similar experiences have you had?
- ◆ What do you think will happen next?
- ◆ What would you do in this situation?
- ◆ If you could change ONE thing in the plot, what would it be and how would it change the story?
- ◆ How would you make the story more real or more imaginative?

Characters

- ◆ How is the main character different from you?
- ◆ Would you want _____ to be one of your friends? Why or why not?
- ◆ Which character is most interesting to you? Why?

Enrichment to the Listening Logs

Level 2: You may want to draw attention to the fact that before the 1920s, writers wrote in longer sentences. Together, count the words in a long sentence or paragraph by Charles Dickens, Herman Melville, or Jane Austen. Compare this to a modern writer such as John Steinbeck (*The Pearl*) or Ernest Hemingway (*The Old Man and the Sea*). Discuss:

- ◆ Are longer sentences more difficult for today's reader? Why?
- ◆ What could you do to make longer sentences and paragraphs easier to read and understand?
- ◆ Would this take away from the style of the author?

Level 3: After reading the high-interest book aloud, go to a classic novel or play, with a plot line that would still be attractive to your learner, but with more advanced language patterns. Discuss:

- ◆ What vocabulary or figures of speech did you hear that you did not understand?
- ◆ How is the writing different from the previous book or from _____?

- How might the main character act in today's world?
- How were people treated differently in this novel than they are today?

▶ ACTIVITIES, ACTIVITIES, ACTIVITIES

These activities promote skills for literary response and expression in all the children in your family. As usual, feel free to adjust these activities to your middle schooler's maturity and abilities.

A Playwright, Right?

Write, produce, and direct a play for your younger siblings or neighbors or younger members of your homeschooling support group, from a book that is a favorite of theirs.

The Next Hemingway?

Pick your favorite story from *The Complete Short Stories of Ernest Hemingway* (Scribner, 1998). Closely mimic the writing style, and craft your own Hemingwayesque story. Extra points for humor!

Story Telling

Don't forget the value of story-telling as a way to nurture any child's verbal and narrative growth. Bright kids can be awesome story weavers! Here are two story-creation games that kids love, especially those linguistic and interpersonal learners:

Complete-the-Story. A simple activity that improves listening skills, comprehension, vocabulary, and creative writing. One person begins to tell a story about any subject. After a few descriptive sentences, that person says, "And then . . . " Anyone listening for the "and then" can jump in, adding a few more details or events to the story, until he or she says "And then . . . " That's when someone else picks up the story. One rule can be that the story must come to a satisfying conclusion at the end of three rounds of play.

The Minister's Cat. An old parlor game where one person starts with "The minister's cat is an *adorable* cat." The second player continues, substituting another adjective that begins with *a*: "The minister's cat is an *aggressive* cat." Play continues until someone cannot think of another *a* word/adjective. If you are playing in a large group, the stumped player exits the game and play continues with *b* words, then *c* words, etc., until only one player is left. In a small group or with young children, the stumped player remains in the game, but loses a turn, and the play continues through each letter (round) of the alphabet. Or, you can give an M&M or a penny to each player who makes it through a round, and if a player runs out of adjectives, he doesn't get the treat for that round.

Literary Debates

Encourage oral debate, or even a formal debate, about literature. For example, students who have read *A Tree Grows in Brooklyn* and *All Creatures Great and Small* can debate which is a better piece of literature and why.

Fairy Tales

Especially effective with visual/spatial learners is writing and illustrating your own fairy tale or fable or myth, using the conventions of the genre.

Moving to the Music

Try moving in the style of animals suggested in the music "Carnival of the Animals" by Camille Saint-Saens. What does the music do to suggest your movements? Discuss this together; for example, "The music sounded slow and low when I was an elephant, smooth and flowing when I was a fish in an aquarium, and uneven and jumpy when I was a kangaroo."

Journaling

Journals are hard to use in institutional school because, to use them correctly, students need feedback regularly, and journals can simply "pile up" without the attention of the teacher. If you want to try journaling, it's a good idea to start it while on a vacation or after a field trip. Have your homeschooler divide his paper vertically with two columns. The left one is titled "What I Saw," and the other one, "What I Thought about What I Saw." Your goal is for your middle schooler to develop introspection and to perhaps see the value in keeping a journal.

Creative Folk Tales

Invent a different oral, narrative form for telling a folk or fairy tale or myth, such as:

- a picture book with poetry
- a puppet show
- a play
- a freshly composed ballad
- a narrated pantomime

Common-Theme Stories

A very challenging enrichment activity is to compile a collection of literature from different cultures around a common theme and write an analytic introduction to the collection explaining the similarities and differences.

Interior/Exterior Boxes

This activity teaches the perceptions of people and self, as with writers and readers. It is best done in a group of eight or more—with writers of all ages, if possible—working apart from each other.

1. Each person brings a box, usually cardboard, that 'fits' his or her personality. Some boxes of unusual shapes can be bought at crafts stores. Boxes may be handmade too.
2. On the *outside* of the box, the each artist glues a collage of pictures and words cut from magazines that describes him as he thinks others see him. Don't peek at each other's boxes as they are being created.

3. Each person then covers the *inside* with pictures and words that describe him as he really is. (Do not put anything that you don't wish to disclose.) Nowhere on the boxes should names be put. Each artist puts his or her box in an opaque bag, with a piece of paper with the student's name on it, and takes it to the leader.

4. The leader puts the boxes out on several tables or around a large room, with a number identifying each box.

5. Writing on notebook paper, the box makers—now writers—move from box to box, writing their description and assessment of the external qualities of the box maker, as portrayed by the exterior of the boxes. They do the same with the interior of the boxes. These comments can be in notes and fragments. Then they make a guess as to whose box it is. For example:

Box #1

Exterior: *There are lots of pictures of possessions in this collage and many colorful flowers and suns faces—this person thinks others see him or her as frivolous and always cheerful, I think,* and so on.

Interior: *Very warm and fuzzy. Dark, dreamy colors show the person is really a romantic and rather shy,* and so on.

Guess who? *Lisa Mitchell*

Note: Writers should not talk to each other or discuss the boxes during this meditative and creative time.

6. The leader gathers and types up the comments on each box (deleting any inappropriate comments) and hands out the compiled comments to each box maker. People may want to discuss their perceptions of themselves and others, depending on the group.

Summary

Often, parents hope that, beyond learning to read, their gifted children will grow up to absorb and connect with literary works, drawing from their expanding personal knowledge and experience, loving to interpret, to analyze, and to create literature as well. In the dual role as parent and teacher, homeschooling parents can instill a love of reading in their children, one that will last a lifetime.

▶ **PRACTICE** *(Keys, examples, and rubrics may be found in Appendix A)*

Note: These practice problems span a range of possibilities for literary response and self-expression. Adapt them to your learner's level of mastery. As elsewhere in this book, these prompts may be read/answered/discussed aloud.

I. Haiku, Anyone?

Research haikus in the library or on the Internet, reading many examples (Remember: 5-7-5 syllables, expressing the senses, often with nature). An excellent book is Harold Tran Stewart's *A Network of Fireflies*. Then consider and collect adjectives about a subject that interests you, such as big cats or space stations. Finally, create as many haikus as pour forth! Get your family to write them too.

Example

> Howl of winter winds,
> Finishing our Scrabble game
> By light of candles.
> —Anne Davidson, Old Orchard Beach, ME
> Published in *Mayfly* magazine, July 2000, www.family-net.net/~brooksbooks/mayfly.html

II. Poem vs. Music vs. Animation

Read the English translation of Goethe's poem "The Sorcerer's Apprentice." This poem was based on an old fairy tale. You can find the poem on the Internet at www.fln.vcu.edu/goethe/zauber_e3.html. Choose one or more of these activities:

Level 1: After reading the poem, sit and imagine the experiences, then write a journal entry describing how *you* would feel as the sorcerer's apprentice.

Level 2: Create an additional poetry verse and chorus of what happens in the poem next, in the style of Goethe.

Level 3: Listen to "The Sorcerer's Apprentice" by French composer Paul Dukas, and compare the experiences of reading the poem and listening to the composition. If you can, rent the video or DVD of Disney's *Fantasia*, and see the animated version and compare all three.

III. Blind/Deaf Experience

In this writing exercise, you spend one hour either "blind" or "deaf" in a safe situation of your choosing. You then write two pages, typewritten: Part I, a narrative about being a blind or deaf person; Part II, exposition about what you learned from the experiment.

A

Answer Key

CHAPTER 2

Page 58 Picturesque Words

Here are a few—among many—possible answers:

1. puppy, cold-nose, mutt, tail-wagger, wolf, fur-ball, hound, mongrel, stray, pooch, poochie, man's best friend, cur, canine, woofy, drool-face, face cleaning machine, beggar, yappy dog, bloodhound, tracker, best of the breed

2. scarlet, coral, blood-red, vermillion, ruby, crimson, cherry red, rust, magenta, fuchsia, lipstick red, rosy red, jelly red, bloodshot, as red as Santa's cheeks, as a bowl of cherries

3. glider, flying greyhound, silver bird, aircraft, flying machine, airliner, jet, shuttle, lighter-than-air machine, rocket, bomber, fighter, airship, seaplane, hydroplane, sky bus

4. amble, take a hike, roam, saunter, skip, hop, move, slide, glide, lope, stride, tread, limp, meander, stroll, march, shuffle, wend your way, do the moonwalk, promenade, trek, tour, hoof it, knock about, cruise, toddle along

5. stash, file, put away, put aside, deposit, amass, pile up, lay away, lay by, lock away, lock up, put in mothballs, salt away

6. female, maid, maiden, chick, bird, miss, madam, lass, skirt, dame, lady, coed, lassie, damsel, babe, tomboy, spinster, Mrs., Ms., debutante, matron, doll, broad, fair sex, female of the species, beauty

Rubrics

Chapter 1 displays one kind of rubric, which serves as a guide for subjective evaluation of writing. Another type of rubric is included in this section. You may prefer one version over the other, or your learner may devise her own.

Use a rubric for your student to grow as a writer, while learning techniques to:

◆ Establish focus by asserting a main or controlling idea
◆ Develop content using sufficient and appropriate supporting details
◆ Provide a logical pattern of organization
◆ Convey a sense of style with the use of varied vocabulary and sentences
◆ Demonstrate control of the conventions of standard written English

For example, here is a rubric for evaluating your learner's narrative writing in her response to "An Object."

SCORE & DESCRIPTION FOR NARRATIVE WRITING

Excellent

- Tells a well-developed story with relevant descriptive details across the response.
- Events are well connected and tie the story together with transitions across the response; narration is interesting.
- Sustains varied sentence structure and exhibits specific word choices.
- Exhibits control over sentence boundaries; errors in grammar, spelling, and mechanics do not interfere with understanding.

Skillful

- Events are connected in much of the response; may lack some transitions.
- Exhibits some variety in sentence structure and exhibits some specific word choices.
- Generally exhibits control over sentence boundaries; errors in grammar, spelling, and mechanics do not interfere with understanding.

Sufficient

- Tells a clear story with little development; has few details.
- Events are generally related; may contain brief digressions or inconsistencies.
- Generally has simple sentences and simple word choice; may exhibit uneven control over sentence boundaries.
- Has sentences that consist mostly of complete, clear, distinct thoughts; errors in grammar, spelling, and mechanics generally do not interfere with understanding.

Uneven

May be characterized by one or more of the following:

- Attempts to tell a story, but tells only part of a story, gives a plan for a story, or is list-like.
- Lacks a clear progression of events; elements may not fit together or be in sequence.
- Exhibits uneven control over sentence boundaries and may have some inaccurate word choices.
- Errors in grammar, spelling, and mechanics sometimes interfere with understanding.

Unsatisfactory

May be characterized by one or more of the following:

- Attempts a response but may only paraphrase the prompt or be extremely brief.
- Exhibits no control over organization.
- Exhibits no control over sentence formation; word choice is inaccurate across the response.
- Characterized by misspellings, missing words, incorrect word order; errors in grammar, spelling, and mechanics severely impede understanding across the response.

Page 58 An Object

Example of an intermediate-to-advanced response:

"And there's a long fly ball—it must be, it could be, it's a home run!" The announcer shouted this out of his small press box above home plate. I was six and I remember everyone in my section standing up and yelling. My hero, Omar Gonzalez, had just hit a home run and it was coming my way. As the ball approached, beer and nachos were flying left and right and everyone was getting all excited. The ball landed onto a pillow held by Cubs fans about three rows below me and almost miraculously bounced off of them and landed perfectly in my tanned Wilson glove.

For weeks I dragged the details of the story on and on, and just when my parents thought they could recite it from memory, I would change it so, for example, I would become a heroic figure instead of just a lucky kid. But that ball, it too changed, just as the story did. I would play catch with the neighborhood kids, and it seemed like the ball would come right to my glove. It almost became a part of me, or at least a good luck charm. Once I realized how important that ball was to me, I placed it on my bookcase shelf and dreamed about it and my dream to play for the Cubs.

As I grew up, I continued to play baseball and was remarkably good, but I began to forget where I'd got that old baseball on the shelf. Slowly I began to dream about other things and my desire was lost somewhere in the past. As playing ball in college became more of a reality, I kept practicing and practicing and eventually made the practice team. I can still remember packing up my gear to go to college, and my mother asked why I didn't take the ball.

"You mean that old thing? Why would I need that?"

"Don't you remember, don't you know where this came from?"

So she retold the story, the actual story. She convinced me to take the ball off with me to school, where I put it in a drawer. I played the worst baseball I had ever played. So I took my mom's advice, and I started playing catch with the ball I had caught at Wrigley Field. Out of nowhere, my skills and talent, but especially my desire, returned. I made the starting line-up and eventually progressed my way into the major leagues.

Now I am an overweight designated hitter on some AA farm team in Iowa. My days in the bigs are over. But on my last at bat as a major league ball player, I hit a home run, and I only pray that the little guy who caught it will never put it up on his shelf.

Comments: *This response is excellent, one where the elements of good writing come together. It is both clear and consistently developed with details, as in the opening description of how the narrator caught the ball. It is well organized; the student moves easily from past to present to describe how the baseball has affected his life and aspirations. The story is so vivid that it seems autobiographical; it seems as if we are having a social conversation with the first-person storyteller; it is surprising to realize at the end that the student has in fact created an older character.*

▶ CHAPTER 3

Page 77 Biography
Research and essays will vary considerably. You might want to consider:

- ◆ Was I surprised by the two people he chose to write about?
- ◆ Did my learner find biographical sources that were interesting to him? That were challenging?
- ◆ Did he explore different types of sources (encyclopedia software, books and magazines, Internet, oral history)?
- ◆ Did he explain how the time in which his choices lived affected their lives in a convincing, original, and well-written manner?

The following clues may help you evaluate your homeschooler's efforts in writing for informational purposes.

Criteria for Informational Language

When writing for information and understanding, ask "What is the message I am communicating?' and "What is the purpose of this information?" You might consider these criteria:

VALID—The facts and data must be accurate, precise, and relevant to the purpose.
VERIFIABLE—Information should be well founded and able to be traced to reliable sources.
PUBLIC—The information must be clear and understandable to a reading or listening audience.
EFFICIENT—The information should be presented concisely.

Page 70 Gender Stereotyping

Some Possible Evaluating Points for #1:
1. Did my learner choose examples that apply to the exercise?
2. Did she describe and tally the ads or illustrations?
3. Does she express the results of her findings clearly and with support?

Some Possible Evaluating Points for #2:

1. Did my learner state his sources?

2. Did he clarify his findings through his comparisons of the two periodicals?

3. Did he state his opinions or keep the report objective? (no right answer here)

Expressing Opinion

When your learner looks to persuade others or to express his opinion, he should ask these guiding questions:

1. Who is my audience?

2. What message do I want to communicate?

3. What is my point of view, my bias?

4. What evidence supports my opinion?

5. What is the best way to convince this particular audience?

6. What kind of response or action am I seeking?

7. How will I evaluate my own writing or speaking?

Practicing Critical Analysis

The following ideas provide more opportunity to practice critical analysis skills. As always, adjust these activities to match the learning styles and mastery level of your homeschooler.

- ◆ Evaluate what you read, write, and hear, especially looking for clarity, good logic, supporting detail, comprehensiveness, and originality.
- ◆ Discuss differences in perspective in the world around us. For example, in considering whether to allow a new industry into your community, one group might be enthusiastic about the additional jobs to be created, while others are concerned about the air and noise pollution that could result.
- ◆ Read a sports editorial and evaluate it together, talking about the criteria of accuracy, objectivity, comprehensiveness, and understanding of the game.
- ◆ Point out examples of propaganda techniques (such as "bandwagon," "plain folks" language, and "sweeping generalities") in public documents and speeches.
- ◆ Analyze points of view, for example, one critic condemning a biography for its length, while another praises its accuracy and never mentions its length.
- ◆ Compare two different literary forms expressing the same theme, such as music lyrics and a story about the loss of a love.
- ◆ Change a first-person account to a textbook-like description of an event or vice versa.

This essay is an ideal opportunity for your learner to be very inventive. Gifted writers may create novel angles, such as:

- making a cake from the viewpoint of a bowl
- explaining the game of baseball to a space traveler
- grass being mowed, raked up, and jumped in from the viewpoint of a nearby cricket
- changing a sound card on a motherboard, written in robot-speak
- describing a visit to the dentist as a cultural anthropologist would

What to evaluate in your learner's narrative?

- point of view
- originality (especially with those creatively gifted)
- opening/closing
- humor
- enthusiasm
- examples and supporting details
- vocabulary appropriate to the task being taught and the method used to teach it
- graphics, maps, cartoons, or sketches appropriate to the task being taught

▶ CHAPTER 4

Page 93 Fantasy Future

Level 1 Example: Imagine this. Soaring through the crisp air, your lungs pleasantly burning with the chill. Your body taut—yet flexible—you are totally fit, as you slalom around the pines, your snowboard careening like a surfboard on ice. Your faithful St. Bernard, Lucy, bounding, keeping pace, a keg of hot chocolate at her neck. Yes, you are part of a snowboarding search-and-rescue team in the Rocky Mountains!

Your duties are to find and help lost skiers, injured athletes, and tourists needing help during a blizzard. Your rewards are obvious: fresh air, the sky, the stunning landscape, and the undying gratitude of dozens!

For Level 2's goal, add to previous example:

I would like to discuss my dream job with the late Sir Ernest Shackleton, English explorer of the South Pole. First I would ask him for details about one of the greatest tales of survival in expedition history, his 1914 voyage to the Antarctic. Just one day's sail from the continent, his ship *Endurance* became trapped in sea ice. Frozen fast for ten months, the ship was crushed and destroyed by ice pressure, and the crew was forced to abandon ship. After camping on the ice for five months,

Shackleton made two open-boat journeys, one of which—a treacherous 800-mile ocean crossing to South Georgia Island—is now considered one of the greatest boat journeys in history.

Trekking across the mountains of South Georgia, Shackleton reached the island's remote whaling station, organized a rescue team, and saved all of the men he had left behind. Shackleton had superb leadership skills evidenced by the fact that he encouraged and bullied 28 fellow explorers to survive against all odds. I would talk with him about survival techniques and show him some of the miracles of modern cold-weather exploration. These would include mylar blankets, below-freezing sleeping bags, waterproof matches, mountaineering tools, heat packs, and freeze dried food. It would be fun to impress such a brilliant man!

For Level 3's goal, add to previous example:

To make this fantasy future come true (unfortunately, without the part about meeting Shackleton), I would start researching snow and ice survival techniques and search-and-rescue operations. I would read everything I could on the subject, taking an S & R course as soon as they would let me in. I would save up to visit a Ranger sub-station in Alaska or Canada. I would ask to be an apprentice rescuer without wages for six months and make myself indispensable! That is how I would achieve my fantasy future.

Page 95 What's in a Name?

Level 1: Answers will vary, but should contain reasons, examples, and detail. If writer uses a persuasive angle, read the section called "Persuasive Writing Rubric" for evaluative goals.

Level 2: Your student may choose and list among these research tools for names:

- Ask a reference librarian
- Check out a large city's phone book
- Internet search engine: "Ten Most Common American Surnames"
- Look in Encarta or another software encyclopedia
- Look it up in the Almanac
- Find books on names and history of names
- Go to www.askjeeves.com

Level 3: Your learner may be lucky to have you and other relatives to talk with about these issues. There may be letters, journals, or photos to peruse. This may lead your reader to family histories, or genealogy. An adopted child may learn the history of his adoptive family and write himself into the family history or draw himself into the family tree. Poems, family folk tales, and drawings should be evaluated on the student's success in turning his research into another affecting art form.

Persuasive Writing Rubric

If your learner uses persuasive writing in any part of these exercise, you may be guided by the comments in the following rubric.

SCORE & DESCRIPTION FOR NARRATIVE WRITING

Excellent
- Takes a clear position, is persuasive, and develops support with well-chosen details, reasons, or examples across the response.
- Is well organized; maintains focus.
- Sustains varied sentence structure and exhibits specific word choices.
- Exhibits control over sentence boundaries; errors in grammar, spelling, and mechanics do not interfere with understanding.

Skillful
- Takes a clear position, is persuasive, and develops support with some specific details, reasons, or examples.
- Provides some organization of ideas; for example, by using contrast or building to a point.
- Exhibits some variety in sentence structure and exhibits some specific word choices.
- Generally exhibits control over sentence boundaries; errors in grammar, spelling, and mechanics do not interfere with understanding.

Sufficient
- Takes a clear position, is somewhat persuasive, with support that is clear and generally related to the issue.
- Is generally organized.
- Generally has simple sentences and simple word choice; may exhibit uneven control over sentence boundaries.
- Has sentences that consist mostly of complete, clear, distinct thoughts; errors in grammar, spelling, and mechanics generally do not interfere with understanding.

Uneven
May be characterized by one or more of the following:
- Takes a position and offers limited or incomplete support; some reasons may not be clear or related to the issue; not very persuasive.
- Is disorganized or provides a disjointed sequence of information.
- Exhibits uneven control over sentence boundaries and may have some inaccurate word choices.
- Errors in grammar, spelling, and mechanics sometimes interfere with understanding.

Unsatisfactory
May be characterized by one or more of the following:
- Takes a position but provides no support, or attempts to take a position (is on topic) but the position is very unclear; not persuasive; may only paraphrase the prompt.
- Exhibits no control over organization.
- Exhibits no control over sentence formation; word choice is inaccurate across the response.
- Characterized by misspellings, missing words, incorrect word order; errors in grammar, spelling, and mechanics severely impede understanding across the response.

▶ CHAPTER 5

Pages 113–114 Haiku, Anyone?

You and your young poet will enjoy these notes by haiku expert Jane Reichhold, from her articles on the Internet. (Type Jane Reichhold into your Internet search engine, or investigate several haiku sites through www.askjeeves.com.) There are many more techniques and samples on Reichhold's pages

The Technique of Comparison   In the words of Betty Drevniok: "In haiku the SOMETHING and the SOMETHING ELSE are set down together in clearly stated images. Together they complete and fulfill each other as ONE PARTICULAR EVENT." She leaves the reader to understand that the idea of comparison is showing how two different things are similar or share similar aspects.

> a spring nap
> downstream cherry trees
> in bud

What is expressed, but not said, is the thought that buds on a tree can be compared to flowers taking a nap. One could also ask, to what other images could cherry buds be compared? A long list of items can form in one's mind and be substituted for the first line. Or one can turn the idea around and ask what in the spring landscape can be compared to a nap without naming things that close their eyes to sleep. By changing either of these images, one can come up with one's own haiku while getting a new appreciation and awareness of comparison.

The Technique of Contrast   Now the job feels easier. All one has to do is to contrast images.

> long hard rain
> hanging in the willows
> tender new leaves

The delight from this technique is the excitement that opposites create. You have instant built-in interest in the most common haiku 'moment.' And yet most of the surprises of life are the contrasts, and therefore this technique is a major one for haiku.

The Technique of Association   This can be thought of as "how different things relate or come together". The Zen of this technique is called "oneness" or showing how everything is part of everything else. You do not have to be a Buddhist to see this; simply being aware of what is, is illumination enough.

> ancestors
> the wild plum
> blooms again

If this is too hard to see because you do not equate your ancestors with plum trees, perhaps it is easier to understand with:

> moving into the sun
> the pony takes with him
> some mountain shadow

Does it help for me to explain how this [hai]ku came to be written? I was watching some ponies grazing early in the morning on a meadow that was still partially covered with the shadow of the mountain. As the grazing pony moved slowly into the sunshine, I happened to be focused on the shadow and actually saw some of the mountain's shadow follow the pony—to break off and become his shadow. It can also be thought that the pony eating the grass of the mountain becomes the mountain and vice versa. When the boundaries disappear between the things that separates them, it is truly a holy moment of insight, and it is no wonder that haiku writers are educated to latch on to these miracles and to preserve them in [hai]ku.

Copyright © Jane Reichhold 2000, as published in the Autumn, 2000 issue of *Frogpond*, Journal of the Haiku Society of America

Page 114 *Poem vs. Music vs. Animation*
By the way, the musical compositions in the Disney movie *Fantasia* are

- *Toccata and Fugue in D Minor* by Johann Sebastian Bach
- *The Nutcracker Suite* by Tchaikovsky
- *The Sorcerer's Apprentice* by Paul Dukas
- *The Rite of Spring* by Igor Stravinsky
- *The Pastoral Symphony* by Ludwig van Beethoven
- *Dance of the Hours* by Amilcare Ponchielli
- *Night on Bald Mountain* by Modeste Moussorgsky
- *Ave Maria* by Franz Shubert

Page 114 *Blind/Deaf Experience*
This exercise is both narrative (your learner's story as a blind or deaf person) and expository (what your learner gained from this experiment). It does require involvement with the topic, which is one of the elements to look for when evaluating.

B

Glossary of Language Arts Terms

*A*lliteration? Diphthong? Find these words and more in this helpful collection of language arts terms.

Abstract A summary of the essential points in writing.

Aesthetic Appreciative of beauty, especially in writing and art.

Affixes One or more sounds or letters attached to the beginning or end of a word or base; also known as prefixes or suffixes.

Alliteration Repetition of the same letter or sound at the beginning of two or more consecutive words near one another; as in *fly o'er waste fens and windy fields*.

Allusions An implied or indirect reference to another person or thing found in another piece of literature or in history; in Western literature, quite often a reference to a figure or event in the Bible or mythology.

Analogy A comparison based upon a resemblance between two things; probably the two most common are the simile and the metaphor.

Antecedent Pronouns are words that take the place of nouns; the antecedent for the pronoun is the noun it takes the place of. For example, "John fell down, but he didn't hurt himself." Here, the pronouns *he* and *himself* take the place of *John*; therefore, John is the antecedent for *he* and *himself*.

Antonyms Words with opposite meanings; for example, *hot* and *cold*.

Appositives A word or phrase that renames the noun or pronoun before it; for example, "John, *an experienced teacher*, serves on several curriculum committees."

Blends Two or more consecutive consonants that begin a syllable, such as *bl*end.

Brainstorming Collecting ideas in groups by freely sharing a large number of possibilities.

Comparative The form of an adjective or adverb used when comparing two things, such as *warmer*, *more beautiful*, or *better*.

Connotation The suggested or emotional meaning of a word; the following words have the same *denotation* (dictionary definition) but their connotations are different: *thin, skinny, slender*.

Conventions The usual rules of grammar, punctuation, and spelling.

CVC A simple spelling pattern—a c̲onsonant, a v̲owel, and a c̲onsonant: *cat*.

Declarative Sentences Sentences that make statements; for example, "Becky is a student."

Decode To recognize and interpret; in this case, in reading words.

Dialects Regional or social varieties of language with vocabulary, grammar, or pronunciation different from other regional or social varieties.

Diphthongs A vowel sound produced when the tongue glides from one vowel to another such as in *bee, bay, toy, buy*.

Environmental Print and other graphic symbols, other than books, found in the physical print environment, such as street signs, billboards, etc.

Exclamatory Sentence Sentence that expresses emotion; for example, "I just qualified for the Olympics!"

Expository The form of non-fiction writing which informs or explains.

Extemporaneous Prepared, but spoken without notes or text.

External Punctuation Punctuation found at the end of a sentence i.e., period, question mark, or exclamation point.

Figurative Language Comparing or identifying one thing with another that has a meaning or connotation familiar to the reader; see *metaphor* or *simile* as examples.

Graphic Organizer A teacher- or student-related tool used to record and organize information when reading, such as a schematic drawing; see *webbing*.

Homographs Words that are spelled the same but have different pronunciations or meanings i.e. the *bow* of a ship and a *bow* and arrow, also called homonyms.

Hyperbole A figure of speech that uses intentional exaggeration: She cried *buckets of tears*.

Hypothesis An assumption made to test its logical consequences.

Idioms An expression used in a language that has a meaning that cannot be derived from the words themselves; an example would be "I ran into Joe the other day." (Here, the meaning is not that you physically "ran into" the other person but that you met him.)

Imperative Sentence Sentences that give commands; for example, "Open your books to page 322."

Impromptu Composed or performed on the spur of the moment.

Inferences Conclusions arrived at by reasoning from evidence.

Informative Paper Any paper that offers information, such as a report or a how-to essay.

Internal Punctuation Punctuation within a sentence, such as commas, semicolons, or apostrophes.

Interrogative Sentence Sentences which ask questions; for example, "Who is that?"

Intonation The rise and fall in pitch of the voice in speech.

Inversion A change in normal word order, such as from "I see the cat" to "The cat I see."

Irony Twisting the meaning of words in ways that create the opposite impression. There are three major types:

Verbal irony: when someone says the opposite of what is meant; for example, "Having the flu is so much fun, isn't it?"

Irony of situation: when there is a discrepancy between what may reasonably be expected to happen in a situation and what actually occurs; for example when Character #1 sets a trap for Character #2 but Character #1 falls into the trap himself.

Dramatic irony: when the reader/audience knows something that the character does not know.

Jargon The technical terminology or characteristic idiom of a special activity or group; for example, people who do not use computers might not know the special computer meaning of such words as *mouse* or *icon* or *megabyte*.

Metaphor An implied comparison between two objects or actions, such as, "The ship knifed through the water" or "The moon was tossed upon cloudy seas" (the action of the ship being compared to the slicing of a knife and the cloudy sky being compared to an ocean with waves); see *simile*.

Modifiers Adjectival and adverbial words, phrases, or clauses.

Multimedia Using different means of communication such as overhead transparencies, flip charts, or audio tapes.

Onomatopoeia The use of a word whose sound suggests the sense of the word, such as *sizzle*, *clang*, or *snap, crackle, and pop*.

Parallelism Ideas in a series are arranged in words, phrases, sentences, or paragraphs that are similar in grammatical structure: Words: "he was left *alone, lonely*, and *heartbroken*" (adjectives). Phrases: " . . . government *of the people, by the people*, and *for the people . . .* " (prepositional phrases).

Paraphrase To read text or listen to an idea and then put in your own words.

Personification Figure of speech in which something that is not human is given human characteristics, such as "The tree lifts its arms to the sky."

Phonics The system by which symbols represent sounds in an alphabetic writing system.

Point of View The perspective from which a story is presented to a reader; the most common are first person, third person singular (or limited), and third person omniscient.

Prose Anything not written in poetry form.

R-Controlled Vowel In English, when an *r* colors the way the preceding vowel is pronounced, such as *bad* and *bar* or *can* and *car*.

Reading Rate The speed at which a selection is read and the manner in which it is read, depending on the purpose; skimming, scanning, studying, or reading for pleasure.

Reflective Texts Writing based on a writer's prior knowledge or experience.

Rhetorical Relating to the art of writing as a means of communication or persuasion.

Rubric Scoring guide; written criteria used to judge a particular kind of performance.

"Showing," not "Telling" Writing that allows the reader to see, hear, touch, taste, or smell what is written. Rather than saying "He was angry," saying "He trembled and pounded his fist on the table, frightening us all."

Simile An explicit comparison between two objects or actions using *like* or *as*, such as "Soft as a feather" or "The cat's tongue feels like sandpaper." See *metaphor*.

Stylistic Devices Techniques of writing used by an author to achieve a purpose, such as diction, detail, or point of view.

Subject/Verb Agreement Using a singular verb with a singular subject or a plural verb with a plural agreement subject.

Subordination The act of putting an idea of lesser importance in a clause that cannot stand alone; for example, "*Because he was late,* he missed the bus."

Superlative Modifier The form of an adjective or adverb used when comparing three or more things, such as *warmest, most beautiful,* or *best.*

Synonyms Words with similar meanings; for example, *pretty* and *beautiful.*

Syntax The way in which words are put together or related to one another in a sentence; "I ate the sandwich." "The sandwich I ate." "Ate I the sandwich?"

Synthesize To combine several sources of ideas in order to produce a coherent whole; a high-level critical-thinking skill.

Theme The dominant idea of a work of literature.

Thesis A proposition to be proved.

Thesis Statement A sentence containing the main idea of a piece of writing.

Topic The subject being written about.

Usage The way words are used correctly in a sentence, such as subject/verb agreement, pronoun/antecedent agreement, or consistency of tense.

Voice The presence of the writer on the page; writing with strong voice leaves the reader feeling a strong connection to the writing and/or writer.

Webbing A prewriting technique that often makes use of circles or squares to organize ideas regarding a topic for writing.

C

Resources for Gifted Learners

▶ Books

The following is a list of recommended books for learners in the middle school years, but you may find that your child reads above or below the level of some books. These titles are a mixture of old classics and new favorites, and include some lists compiled by middle schoolers of books they've especially liked. They can be found at your local library or bookstore, or ordered online from sites like Powells.com or BookSense.com.

Fiction and Literature

Alcott, Louisa May. *Little Women*
Babbitt, Natalie. *Tuck Everlasting*
Bauer, Joan. *Hope Was Here*
Block, Francesca Lia. *Girl Goddess #9*
Burnett, Frances Hodgson. *The Secret Garden*
Cisneros, Sandra. *The House on Mango Street*
Cormier, Robert. *The Chocolate War*
Dorris, Michael. *Morning Girl*
George, Jean Craighead. *My Side of the Mountain*
Hinton, S.E. *The Outsiders*
Juster, Norman. *The Phantom Tollbooth*
Knowles, John. *A Separate Peace*
L'Engle, Madeleine. *A Wrinkle in Time*
Lowry, Lois. *Number the Stars*
Lowry, Lois. *The Giver*
Potok, Chaim. *The Chosen*

Paterson, Katherine. *Lyddie*

Rowling, J.K. *Harry Potter and the Sorcerer's Stone.*

Smith, Betty. *A Tree Grows in Brooklyn*

Smith, Dodie. *I Capture the Castle*

Taylor, Mildred. *Roll of Thunder, Hear My Cry*

Townsend, Sue. *The Secret Diary of Adrian Mole, Aged 13¾*

Biography/Autobiography

Angelou, Maya. *I Know Why the Caged Bird Sings*

Frank, Anne. *The Diary of a Young Girl*

Rosen, Michael. *Shakespeare: His Work and His World*

Wright, Richard. *Black Boy*

Writing

Goldberg, Natalie. *Writing Down the Bones*

Hanson, Anne. *Visual Writing: Diagramming Your Ideas To Communicate Effectively*

Rae, Colleen. *Movies in the Mind: How to Build a Short Story*

Social Studies/History

Bachrach, Susan. *Tell Them We Remember: The Story of The Holocaust*

Beals, Melba. *Warriors Don't Cry: A Searing Memoir of the Battle to Integrate Little Rock's Central High*

Brandenburg, J. *Sand and Fog: Adventures in Southern Africa*

Coleman, Penny. *Rosie the Riveter*

D'Aulaire, Ingri and Edgar. *D'Aulaire's Book of Greek Myths*

Dash, Joan. *We Shall Not Be Moved*

Hoose, Phillip M. *We Were There, Too!: Young People in U.S. History*

Houston, Jeanne Wakatsuki. *Farewell to Manzanar: A True Story of Japanese American Experience During and After the World War II Internment*

Jiang, Ji-Li. *Red Scarf Girl*

Metzer, Milton. *Brother, Can You Spare a Dime?: The Great Depression 1929–1933*

Morin, Isobel. *Our Changing Constitution*

Racine, Ned. *Visual Communication: Understanding Maps, Charts, Diagrams, and Schematics*

WEBSITES

Note: At the time of publication, the websites listed here were current. Due to the ever-changing nature of the Web, we cannot guarantee their continued existence or content. Parents should always supervise their children while they are on the Internet.

Homeschool-Related Web Resources

Apricot Pie: www.apricotpie.com. Message boards, chat, and articles written by and for teen homeschoolers.

Homeschool Teens and College—Homeschooled Teenagers' Web Sites: www.homeschoolteens-college.net/teenwebs.htm.

General Web Resources

Internet Public Library Teen Division: www.ipl.org/teen. Links to teen-friendly websites of all kinds, selected by a librarian and teen advisory panel.

Teen Hoopla: www.ala.org/teenhoopla. Maintained by the American Library Association, this site offers book reviews, message boards, and links to websites created by and for teenagers.

TeenLit Writer's Workshop: www.teenlit.com/workshop. Advice and links to other resources for young writers on topics including punctuation, overcoming writer's block, editing marks, and avoiding clichés.

Hot Popcorn: www.hotpopcorn.com. If your child loves movies, music, and television, this is a great site for her to sound off. Visitors can write their own reviews of movies, as well as get all the latest entertainment news.

The Jason Project: www.jasonproject.org. Homeschoolers can register to follow Dr. Robert Ballard—who discovered the RMS *Titanic*—and his crew on their deep sea expeditions. The project includes print curricula, live satellite broadcasts and video supplements.

Exploratorium: www.exploratorium.edu. The famous San Francisco museum by the same name hosts this site. The museum is dedicated to science, art, and human perception. Here you will find exhibitions from the museum, activities, and resources for projects.

Los Angeles County Museum of Art: www.lacma.org. The Los Angeles County Museum of Art features works of art online. There is also a feature that allows your teen to offer his opinion about a work of art.

Metropolitan Museum of Art: www.metmuseum.org. New York's Metropolitan Museum of Art features 5,000 years of artwork. This is an amazing site that will help your child to find information about art and artists throughout history.

Roots & Shoots: http://vax.wcsu.edu/cyberchimp/roots/rsindex.html. Learn how the Roots & Shoots program teaches young people about environmental awareness and community service—and then join up yourself!

Surf Monkey: www.surfmonkey.com. The content on this site is sure to please your child. Their wonderful links are organized by categories such as *playful, artsy, brainy, spacey, newsworthy, techie, worldly,* and *starstruck.*

Educational Videos/DVDs

Your child's favorite movies are probably not documentaries or nature films—but educational videos don't have to be boring! For a selection of smart, teen-friendly films that you and your child can watch together and discuss, visit the documentary section of your video store, or check out these resources:

The American Library Association's Young Adult Library Services Association (YALSA) selects a list of outstanding videos for young adults each year. The committee that selects the videos is a mixture of teenagers and youth librarians. Past selections have ranged from "Triumph of the Nerds," a biography of Bill Gates, to "Rights from the Heart," a series of vignettes examining the issue of human rights around the world. View current and past recommendations online at www.ala.org/yalsa/booklists/video.

ClassroomVisuals.com (www.classroomvisuals.com) is a mail-order video site. For an annual fee, you can order five videos at a time, for two weeks' viewing, postage paid both ways, delivered to and picked up from your front step. This site lists thousands of videos, both educational and entertaining—from PBS and the Discovery and History channels to biographies to movie classics.

Audio Resources

August House Audio (www.augusthouse.com) publishes a wonderful variety of storytellers on CD and cassette for all ages.

See the American Library Association's selection of the best audio books for young adults at www.ala.org/yalsa/booklists/audio.

Boomerang! is a monthly 70-minute audio magazine for, by, and about kids (800-333-7858)

Audio Memory (www.audiomemory.com) uses music to help kids learn math, geography, history, and much more.

If you have a fast Internet connection, it's even possible to download full-length audio books in Real Audio or MP3 format, sometimes at no charge. To see what's available, visit www.mp3lit.com or broadcast.yahoo.com.

And for great music and interesting commentary, try tuning in to your local public radio station. A listing of stations by city or zip code is available at www.npr.org.

Online Reading Lists for Middle Schoolers

Carol Hurst's Children's Literature Site: www.carolhurst.com. A huge number of book listings with capsules and ratings. Searchable by author, age group, and curriculum area.

The Children's Literature Web Guide: Internet Resources Related to Books for Children and Young Adults: www.acs.ucalgary.ca/~dkbrown. Links, discussion boards, commentary, and recommendations for all ages.

Lion's House Middle and High School Reading List: www.lionshouse.org/education/bl.htm. Focuses mostly on well-known "classic" books, with helpful links to online versions of the books where available.

Teen Reads: www.teenreads.com. Aimed at a teenage audience, this site features reviews by teenagers, book lists, message boards, author interviews, and a weekly newsletter.

For more suggestions, visit the American Library Association's book lists at www.ala.org/yalsa/booklists/index.html.

Resources for Parents

▶ BOOKS ON LANGUAGE ARTS AND GIFTEDNESS

Albert, David H. *And the Skylark Sings with Me: Adventures in Homeschooling and Community-Based Education.* (Gabriola Island, British Columbia: New Society Publishers, 1999).

Alvino, James. *Parents' Guide to Raising A Gifted Child.* (New York: Ballantine, 1996).

Baskin, Barbara, and Karen Harris. *Books for the Gifted Child.* (New York: Bowker, 1980).

Clark, Barbara. *Growing Up Gifted: Developing the Potential of Children at Home and at School,* 5th Edition. (New York: Prentice Hall, 1997).

Feldman, David, and Lynn Goldsmith. *Nature's Gambit: Child Prodigies and The Development of Human Potential.* (New York: Basic Books, 1986).

Galbraith, Judy. *The Gifted Kids' Survival Guide: A Teen Handbook.* (Minneapolis, MN: Free Spirit, 1996).

Gallo, Donald. *From Hinton to Hamlet: Building Bridges Between Young Adult Literature and the Classics.* (Westport, CT: Greenwood, 1996).

Grost, Audrey. *Genius in Residence.* (Englewood Cliffs, NJ: Prentice-Hall, 1970).

Halsted, Judith. *Guiding Gifted Readers: From Preschool through High School.* (Columbus, OH: Ohio Psychology, 1988).

Hauser, Paul, and Gail Nelson. *Books for the Gifted Child (Volume 2).* (New York: Bowker, 1988).

Hynes, Arleen, and Mary Hynes-Berry. *Bibliotherapy: The Interactive Process: A Handbook.* (Boulder, CO: Westview, 1986).

Knight, Bruce Allen, and Stan Bailey. *Parents as Lifelong Teachers of The Gifted.* (West Auckland, New Zealand: Hawker Brownlow, 1997).

Meckstroth, Elizabeth, et al. *Guiding the Gifted Child: A Practical Source for Parents and Teachers.* (Evanston, IL: Great Expectations, 1989).

Rivero, Lisa, and Maurice Fisher. *Gifted Education Comes Home: A Case for Self-Directed Homeschooling.* (Manassas, VA: Gifted Education Press, 2000).

Rivero, Lisa. *Creative Home Schooling for Gifted Children: A Resource Guide.* (Scottsdale, AZ: Great Potential, 2002).

Saunders, Jaquelyn, et al. *Bringing Out the Best: A Resource Guide for Parents of Young Gifted Children.* (Minneapolis, MN: Free Spirit, 1991).

Sganga, Francis T. *Essential Mathematics for Gifted Students: Preparation for Algebra, Grades 4–8.* (Manassas, VA: Gifted Education Press, 2002).

Smutny, Joan, et al. *Stand Up for Your Gifted Child: How to Make the Most of Kids' Strengths at School and at Home.* (Minneapolis, MN: Free Spirit, 2000).

Whitehead, Robert. *A Guide to Selecting Books for Children.* (Metuchen, NJ: Scarecrow, 1984).

▶ Books on Homeschooling

Beechick, Ruth. *You Can Teach Your Child Successfully: Grades 4–8.* (Pollock Pines, CA: Arrow Press, 1992).

Brainerd, Lee, et al. *Basic Skills for Homeschooling: Language Arts and Math for the Middle School Years.* (New York: LearningExpress, 2002).

Cohen, Cafi. *Homeschooling: The Teen Years: Your Complete Guide to Successfully Homeschooling the 13- To 18-Year Old.* (Roseville, CA: Prima Publishing, 2000).

Delisle, James. *Once Upon a Mind: Stories and Scholars of Gifted Child Education.* (New York: Wadsworth, 1999).

Field, Christine. *Help for the Harried Homeschooler: A Practical Guide to Balancing Your Child's Education With the Rest of Your Life.* (Colorado Springs, CO: Harold Shaw, 2002).

Griffith, Mary. *Homeschooling Handbook.* 2nd Edition (Roseville, CA: Prima Publishing, 1999).

Guterson, David. *Family Matters: Why Homeschooling Makes Sense.* (New York: Harvest Books, 1993).

Hendrickson, Borg. *How to Write a Low-Cost/No-Cost Curriculum for Your Home-School Child.* (Sheridan, WY: Mountain Meadow Press, 1998).

Henry, Shari. *Homeschooling: The Middle Years: Your Complete Guide to Successfully Homeschooling the 8- To 12-Year Old Child.* (Roseville, CA: Prima Publishing, 1999).

Keith, Diane Flynn. *Carschooling: Over 500 Entertaining Games & Activities to Turn Travel Time into Learningtime.* (Roseville, CA: Prima, 2002).

Leppert, Mary et al. *Homeschooling Almanac 2002–2003.* (Roseville, CA: Prima Publishing, 2001).

Llewellyn, Grace, ed. *Real Lives: Eleven Teenagers Who Don't Go to School.* (Eugene, OR: Lowry House, 1993).

Llewellyn, Grace. *The Teenage Liberation Handbook: How to Quit School and Get a Real Life and Education.* (Eugene, OR: Lowry House, 1998).

Ransom, Martha. *Complete Idiot's Guide to Homeschooling.* (New York: Alpha Books, 2001).

Rupp, Rebecca. *The Complete Home Learning Source Book.* (New York: Three Rivers Press, Random House, 1998).

Rupp, Rebecca. *Home Learning Year by Year: How to Design a Homeschool Curriculum from Preschool Through High School.* (New York: Three Rivers Press, Random House, 2000).

▶ SELECTED ARTICLES ON LANGUAGE ARTS AND GIFTEDNESS

Boyer, A. "Surviving the blessing: Parenting the highly gifted child." *Understanding our Gifted.* 1 (3), 5, 17, 20–21.

Dirks, J. "Parents' reactions to identification of the gifted." *Roeper Review.* 2 (2), 9–10.

Emerick, Linda J. "Academic underachievement among the gifted: Students' perceptions of factors that reverse the pattern." *Gifted Child Quarterly.* 36(1992):140–146.

Halsted, Judith Wynn. "Guiding the gifted reader." *ERIC Digest #E481.* Published online at www.hearte.com/gasp/481.htm, cited on 04/23/02.

Hawkins, Sue. "Reading Interests of Gifted Children." *Reading Horizons*, 1983. 24.

Hebert, Thomas. "Meeting the affective needs of bright boys through bibliotherapy." *Roeper Review.* 13:207–212.

"Home sweet school." *Time*, Oct. 31, 1994, 62–63.

"In a class of their own." *Newsweek*, Jan. 10, 1994, 58.

American Association for Gifted Children Newsletter, January 1996, vol. III no. 1.

Kearney, Kathi. "Home schooling gifted children." *Understanding Our Gifted* 1 (3), 1, 12–13, 15–16.

Kearny, Kathi. "At home in Maine: gifted children and home schooling." *Gifted Child Today.* May/June, 15–19.

Kearny, Kathi. "Homeschooling gifted children." *Understanding Our Gifted.* 1(3); 1, 12–13, 15–16.

Kline, Bruce, and Meckstroth, Elizabeth. "Understanding and encouraging the exceptionally gifted." *Roeper Review.* 8 (1), 24–30.

Koopmans-Dayton, Jill, and Feldhusen, John. "A resource guide for parents of gifted preschoolers." *Gifted Child Today.* Nov/Dec, 2–7.

Lewis, G. "Alternatives to acceleration for the highly gifted child." *Roeper Review.* 6 (3), 133–136.

McMillan, B.D. "Home education for gifted children." *Gifted Child Today.* Nov/Dec, 55–56.

Silverman, Linda, and Kearney, Kathi. "Parents of the extraordinarily gifted." *Advanced Development.* 1, 41–56.

Silverman, Linda. "The highly gifted." In J. F. Feldhusen, J. VanTassel-Baska, and K. R. Seeley (eds.), *Excellence in Educating Gifted & Talented Learners* (pp. 71–83). Denver: Love.

Tolan, Stephanie. "An open letter to parents, teachers and others: From parents of an exceptionally gifted child." In Webb, James, Meckstroth, Elizabeth, and Tolan, Stephanie, *Guiding the Gifted Child.* Columbus, OH: Ohio Psychology Publishing Co.

Tolan, Stephanie. "Stop accepting, start demanding!" *Gifted Child Monthly* 6 (1), p.6.

Tolan, Stephanie. "Stuck in another dimension: The exceptionally gifted child in school." *Gifted Child Today.* (41), 22–26.

▶ PERIODICALS ON HOMESCHOOLING

Home Education Magazine (6 issues/year)
P.O. Box 1083
Tonasket, WA 98855-1083
800-236-3278
www.home-ed-magazine.com

Home Educator's Family Times (6 issues/year)
www.homeeducator.com/FamilyTimes
(subscriptions to the print version are also available.)

The Link, A Homeschool Newspaper (bi-monthly, no cost)
587 North Ventu Park Road, Suite F-911
Newbury Park, CA 91320
888-470-4513
www.homeschoolnewslink.com

At Home in America—newsletter produced by Homeschool Associates
25 Adams Avenue
Lewiston, ME 04240
207-777-1700
www.athomeinamerica.com

▶ PERIODICALS ON GIFTEDNESS

Gifted Child Today (quarterly)
Prufrock Press
P.O. Box 8813
Waco, TX 76714-8813
www.prufrock.com/mag_gct.html

Gifted Child Quarterly
National Association for Gifted Children
1707 L Street NW, Suite 550
Washington, DC 20036
www.nagc.org/Publications/GiftedChild

Gifted Education Communicator (quarterly)
California Association for the Gifted
15141 East Whittier Boulevard, Suite 510
Whittier, CA 90603
www.cagifted.org/com.htm

Parenting for High Potential (quarterly)
National Association for Gifted Children
1707 L Street NW, Suite 550
Washington, DC 20036
www.nagc.org/Publications/Parenting

Roeper Review (quarterly)
P.O. Box 329
Bloomfield Hills, MI 48303
www.roeperreview.org

Understanding Our Gifted
Open Space Communications
P.O. Box 18268
Boulder, CO 80308
www.openspacecomm.com

▶ WEB RESOURCES ON GIFTEDNESS

Gifted & talented resources at the Virtual School for the Gifted:
   www.vsg.edu.au/resources/default.htm
Gifted Canada—information for gifted children and their parents, primarily of interest to those living in Canada:
   www3.bc.sympatico.ca/giftedcanada/page6.html
Internet Resources for Homeschooling Gifted Students, compiled by gifted education instructor Kathi Kearney:
   www.gifteddevelopment.com/Articles/Homeschool_Int_Res.htm
A to Z Home's Cool—an annotated list of links to online resources on homeschooling gifted kids:
   www.gomilpitas.com/homeschooling/weblinks/gifted.htm
ERIC's Homeschooling Resources for Gifted Students:
   http://ericec.org/minibibs/eb18.html
The Queensland Association for Gifted and Talented Children—this Australian group has compiled a list of links and resources that are of use to anyone working with a gifted child:
   www.qagtc.org.au/bookmark.htm
GT World—links to Web resources on giftedness, as well as recommended reading for parents and gifted adults:
   www.gtworld.org/links.html
An annotated bibliography on homeschooling and giftedness, compiled by gifted education instructor Kathi Kearney:
   http://members.aol.com/discanner/gifthome.html
Hoagies Gifted Education—an all-encompassing gifted education site, featuring information on traditional schooling, special needs learners, resources, and special areas for homeschoolers:
   www.hoagiesgifted.org.
Also check out Hoagies Kids (www.hoagieskids.org), a collection of kid-friendly links with an emphasis on challenging, interesting material.

▶ WEB RESOURCES ON HOMESCHOOLING

The Busy Person's Guide to Homeschooling Grades 7–12: www.wz.com/education/HomeSchoolingGrades7to12.html. A collection of links to web resources, rated and reviewed by homeschoolers.
California Homeschool Network Curriculum and Resource List: www.californiahomeschool.net/resources/links/online.asp. A variety of books, websites and other resources for curriculum development and other homeschooling needs.
Design-a-Study Guides: www.designastudy.com. Everything you need to know to design your own unit study or create a custom curriculum.
Eclectic Homeschool Online: www.eho.org. An online magazine for creative homeschoolers.
Family Unschoolers Network: www.unschooling.org. Resources and support for unschooling, homeschooling, and self-directed learning.

Finding Homeschool Support on the Internet—Freeware and Shareware: www.geocities.com/ Athens/8259/sware.html. Annotated listing of places to find free or low-cost educational computer programs online.

Homefires: The Journal of Homeschooling Online: www.homefires.com. This site by a homeschooling parent provides many new approaches to homeschooling—among them Carschooling®, a collection of resources and teaching methods that can be used while traveling.

Homeschool.com: Your Virtual Home School: www.homeschool.com. Online courses, resource guide, support groups, and message boards.

Homeschool Teens and College: www.homeschoolteenscollege.net. Articles, reviews, and product advice for parents who are homeschooling children from 11 to 18.

Learn in Freedom!: www.learninfreedom.org. Extensive bibliographies, articles, and subject-specific resource guides from homeschoolers and unschoolers.

Multiple Intelligences—Inventory and Informational Site. www.surfaquarium.com/im.htm. Information on the many types of intelligence and learning styles children possess, many of which are frequently undervalued in traditional schools.

The On-Line Books Page: http://digital.library.upenn.edu/books. An index of over 14,000 books which are freely available on the Internet.

PEP: Parents, Educators and Publishers: www.microweb.com/pepsite. Lots of information on children's software programs.

E

Homeschooling Parents' Organizations

One of the best resources for a homeschooling parent is the support, knowledge, and advice of other homeschooling families. This list of national, state, and local homeschooling parents' groups will help you get an idea of the kinds of organizations that are available to you. This list is not comprehensive, but is designed to give you a start in networking with other families in your area.

▶ GIFTED ADVOCACY GROUPS

American Association for Gifted Children—at
  Duke University
P.O. Box 90270
Durham, NC 27708-0270
919-783-6152
www.aagc.org

National Association for Gifted Children
1707 L Street NW, Suite 550
Washington, DC 20036
202-785-4268
www.nagc.org

The National Foundation for Gifted and
  Creative Children
395 Diamond Hill Road
Warwick, RI 02886-8554
401-738-0937
www.nfgcc.org

World Council for Gifted and Talented Children,
  Inc.
18401 Hiawatha Street
Northridge, CA 91326
818-368-7501

▶ NATIONAL HOMESCHOOLING PARENTS' ORGANIZATIONS

Alternative Education Resource Organization
  (AERO)
417 Roslyn Road
Roslyn Heights, NY 11577
www.edrev.org

American Homeschool Association
P.O. Box 3142
Palmer, AK 99645
800-236-3278
www.americanhomeschoolassociation.org

National Challenged Homeschoolers Associated
  Network
P.O. Box 39
Porthill, ID 83853
208-267-6246
www.nathhan.com

National Home Education Network
P.O. Box 41067
Long Beach, CA 90853
www.nhen.org

National Home Education Research Institute
P.O. Box 13939
Salem, OR 97309
503-364-1490
www.nhen.org

▶ STATE/LOCAL HOMESCHOOLING PARENTS' ORGANIZATIONS

Alabama
Baldwin Regional Association of Independent
  Non-Traditional Schools
P.O. Box 1765
Bay Minette, AL 36507-1765
brain@firehousemail.com

North Alabama Home Educators
nahe@geocities.com
www.northalabamahomeeducators.freeservers.
  com

Alaska
Alaska Homeschool Network
www.akhomeschool.net

Arizona
Active Arizona Homeschoolers
4101 West Mulberry Drive
Phoenix, AZ 85019
www.members.tripod.com/home4school

Arizona Families for Home Education
www.afhe.org

Arkansas
Home Educators of Arkansas
P.O. Box 192455
Little Rock, AR 72219
www.geocities.com/Heartland/Garden/4555

California

California Coalition for People for Alternative
Learning Situations (CC-Pals)
P.O. Box 92
Escondido, CA 92025

California Homeschool Network
P.O. Box 55485
Hayward, CA 94545
800-327-5339
www.californiahomeschool.net

HomeSchool Association of California
P.O. Box 868
Davis, CA 95617
888-HSC-4440
www.hsc.org

Colorado

Boulder County Home Educators' Association
www.bchea.com

Colorado Springs Homeschool Support Group
P.O. Box 26117
Colorado Springs, CO 80936-6117
719-598-2636
www.hschool.com

Connecticut

Connecticut Home Educators' Association
203-781-8569
www.cthomeschoolers.com

Delaware

Delaware Home Education Association
P.O. Box 268
Hartly, DE 19953
dheaonline.org

Florida

Florida Parent Educators Association
800-ASK-FPEA
www.fpea.com

West Florida Home Education Support League
P.O. Box 11720
Pensacola, FL 32524-1720
850-981-1222
www.wfhesl.org

Georgia

Home Education Information Resource
P.O. Box 2111
Roswell, GA 30077-2111
404-681-4347
www.heir.org

Hawaii

Hawaii Homeschoolers Association
P.O. Box 893513
Mililani, HI 96789
808-944-3339
www.hawaiihomeschoolassociation.org

Idaho

Idaho Coalition of Home Educators
5415 Kendall Street
Boise, ID 83706
www.iche-idaho.org

Illinois

Grassroots Homeschoolers
918 Princeton Avenue
Matteson, IL 60443
www.grassrootshs.tripod.com

Illinois Home Oriented Unique Schooling
Experience (HOUSE)
www.illinoishouse.org

Indiana

Life Education and Resource Network (LEARN)
www.bloomington.in.us/~learn

Iowa

Iowans Dedicated to Educational Alternatives
  (IDEA)
P.O. Box 17
Teeds Grove, IA 52771
http://home.plutonium.net/~pdiltz/idea

Kansas

Central Kansas Home Educators
Route 1, Box 130
Lyons, KS 67554
316-897-6631

Midwest Parent Educators
P.O. Box 14391
Lenexa, KS 66285-4391
913-791-8089
www.mpekc.org

Kentucky

Kentucky Home Education Association
P.O. Box 81
Winchester, KY 40392-0081
www.khea.8k.com

Louisiana

Louisiana Home Education Network
PMB 700602 West Prien Lake Road
Lake Charles, LA 70601
www.la-home-education.com

Maine

Homeschool Support Network
P.O. Box 708
Gray, ME 04039
888-300-8434
www.homeeducator.com/HSN

Maine Home Education Association
c/o Vicky Packard
10 Willowdale Drive
Gorham, ME 04038
www.geocities.com/mainehomeed

Maryland

Family Unschoolers Network/North County
  Home Educators
1688 Belhaven Woods Court
Pasadena, MD 21122-3727
www.iqcweb.com/nche

Maryland Home Education Association
9085 Flamepool Way
Columbia, MD 21045
410-730-0073
www.mhea.com

Massachusetts

Cape Cod Homeschoolers
P.O. Box 1735
Onset, MA 02558
www.capecodhomeschoolers.com

The Family Resource Center
19 Cedarview Street
Salem, MA 01970
978-741-7449
www.familyrc.com

Homeschooling Together
c/o Sophia Sayigh
24 Avon Place
Arlington, MA 02474
www.homeschoolingtogether.org

Massachusetts Home Learning Association
www.mhla.org

Pathfinder Center
256 North Pleasant Street
Amherst, Massachusetts 01002
413-253-9412
www.pathfindercenter.org

Michigan
Michigan Homeschoolers
www.michiganhomeschoolers.homestead.com

Michigan Learning in Family Environment
   (L.I.F.E.)
www.geocities.com/Heartland/Trail/3405

Minnesota
Minnesota Homeschoolers' Alliance
P.O. Box 23072
Richfield, MN 55423
612-288-9662/888-346-7622
www.homeschoolers.org

Mississippi
Home Educators of Central Mississippi
c/o Alan Bowen
1500 Beverly Drive
Clinton, MS 39056-3507
www2.netdoor.com/~nfgcgrb

Missouri
Families for Home Education
P.O. Box 800
Platte City, MO 64079-0800
www.fhe-mo.org

St. Louis Homeschool Network
c/o Karen Karabell
4147 West Pine
St. Louis, MO 63108
314-534-1171

St. Louis Secular Homeschoolers Co-Op
www.stlsecularhomeschool.org

Montana
Bozeman Homeschool Network
8799 Huffman Lane
Bozeman, MT 59715
406-586-1025

Montana Coalition of Home Educators
P.O. Box 43
Gallatin Gateway, MT 59730
www.mtche.org

Nevada
Homeschool Melting Pot
1000 N. Green Valley Pkwy. #440-231
Henderson, NV 89014
702-320-4840
www.angelfire.com/nv/homeschoolmeltingpot

Northern Nevada Home Schools, Inc.
P.O. Box 21323
Reno, NV 89515
775-852-NNHS
www.angelfire.com/nv/NNHS

New Hampshire
Homeschooling Friends
204 Brackett Road
New Durham, NH 03855-2330
www.homeschoolingfriends.org

New Hampshire Homeschooling Coalition
P.O. Box 2224
Concord, NH 03302
www.nhhomeschooling.org

New Jersey
Homeschoolers Support Network
P.O. Box 56198
Trenton, NJ 08638-7198
www.homeschoolsupport.org

New Jersey Homeschool Association
P.O. Box 1386
Medford, NJ 08055
www.geocities.com/Athens/Agora/3009

Unschoolers Network
2 Smith Street
Farmingdale, NJ 07727
908-938-2473

New Mexico
New Mexico Family Educators
P.O. Box 92776
Albuquerque, NM 87199-2276
505-275-7053

New York
Alliance for Parental Involvement in Education
   (AllPIE)
P.O. Box 59
East Chatham, NY 12060
www.croton.com/allpie

Home Education Exchange of the Southern
   Tier
P.O. Box 85
Southview Station
Binghamton, NY 13903-0085
www.members.tripod.com/~hee

New York City Home Educators Alliance
336 W. 95th Street, #42
New York, NY 10025
www.nychea.com

Tri-County Homeschoolers
37 Birch Drive
Hopewell Junction, NY 12533
www.croton.com/home-ed

North Carolina
Families Learning Together
1670 NC 33 WEST
Chocowinity, NC 27817
www.fltnc.cjb.net

Ohio
Ohio Home Educators Network
P.O. Box 38132
Olmsted Falls, OH 44138-8132
www.ohiohomeeducators.net

Oklahoma
Home Educators' Resource Network (HERO)
   of Oklahoma
302 North Coolidge
Enid, OK 73703-3819
www.oklahomahomeschooling.org

Oregon
Homeschool Information & Services Network
   (HIS Net)
1044 Bismark
Klamath Falls, OR 97601
www.efn.org/~hisnet

Oregon City Public Schools Linkup
(A Parent Designed and Monitored Program
   for Homeschooling Families)
1404 Seventh Street
Oregon City, OR 97045
503-657-2434
www.linkup.orecity.k12.or.us

Oregon Home Education Network
P.O. Box 218
Beaverton, OR 97075-0218
503-321-5166
www.teleport.com/~ohen

Pennsylvania

Pennsylvania Home Education Network
285 Allegheny Street
Meadville, PA 16335
www.phen.org

Pennsylvania Home School Connection
c/o Wendy Bush
650 Company Farm Road
Aspers, PA 17304
717-528-8850
www.homeschoolheadlines.com/hspa.htm

Rhode Island

S.O.S. (Secular in the Ocean State) for Home
   Schoolers
55 West Log Bridge Road
Coventry, RI 02816
401-392-3386

South Carolina

South Carolina Association of Independent
   Home Schools
P.O. Box 2104
Irmo, SC 29063-2104
803-551-1003
www.members.aol.com/scaihs/scaihs.htm

South Dakota

South Dakota Home School Association
P.O. Box 882
Sioux Falls, SD 57101
www.southdakotahomeschool.com

Tennessee

Eclectic Homeschoolers of Tennessee
3135 Lakeland Drive
Nashville, TN 37214
615-889-4938
learninghappens@home.com

Tennessee Home Education Association
P.O. Box 681652
Franklin, TN 37068
858-623-7899
www.tnhea.org

Texas

Houston Alternative Education Alliance
   (HAEA)
P.O. Box 11280
Houston, TX 77293
281-590-3688

Houston Unschoolers Group
www.geocities.com/mhfurgason

Utah

Utah Home Education Association
P.O. Box 737
Farmington, UT 84025
www.utah-uhea.org

Vermont

Vermont Association of Home Educators
214 VT Route 11 West
Chester, VT 05143
802-234-6804
www.vermonthomeschool.org

Virginia

Virginia Home Education Association
P.O. Box 5131
Charlottesville, VA 22905
540-832-3578
www.vhea.org

Washington

Teaching Parents Association
P.O. Box 1934
Woodinville, WA 98072-1934
206-654-5658
www.washtpa.org

Washington Homeschool Organization
6632 S. 191st Place, Suite E-100
Kent, WA 98032-2117
425-251-0439
www.washhomeschool.org

West Virginia
West Virginia Home Educators Association
P.O. Box 3707
Charleston, W.V. 25337
800-736-WVHE
www.wvheahome.homestead.com

Wisconsin
Wisconsin Parents Association
P.O. Box 2502
Madison, WI 53701-2502
608-283-3131
www.homeschooling-wpa.org

Washington, D.C.
Bolling Area Home Educators
http://members.truepath.com/bahe

Puerto Rico and U.S. Virgin Islands
T'CHERs
P.O. Box 867
Boqueron, PR 00622
www.geocities.com/tchers2001

▶ WEB RESOURCES FOR FINDING A SUPPORT GROUP

About.com listings: http://homeschooling.
about.com/cs/supportgroups
A to Z Home's Cool: www.gomilpitas.com/
homeschooling/weblinks/support.htm

Homeschool Resource Page: www.
midnightbeach.com/hs

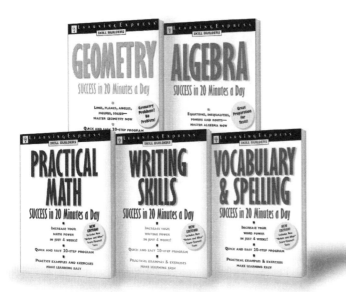